*The most important right we have is the right to be responsible.*

Gerald Amos

Vincent Stanley with Yvon Chouinard

# The Future of the Responsible Company

## What We've Learned from Patagonia's First 50 Years

**patagonia**®

# The Future of the Responsible Company

Patagonia publishes a select list of titles on wilderness, wildlife, and outdoor sports that inspire and restore a connection to the natural world and encourage action to combat climate chaos.

© 2023 Vincent Stanley and Yvon Chouinard

Published by Patagonia Works

Softcover Edition.

Printed in Canada on Rolland Enviro 100 Satin FSC certified 100 percent postconsumer-waste paper.

Softcover ISBN 978-1-952338-11-3
E-Book ISBN 978-1-952338-12-0
Library of Congress Control Number
  2023839943

Editor - John Dutton
Photo Editor - Jane Sievert
Art Director/Designer - Christina Speed
Project Manager - Sonia Moore
Photo Production - Taylor Norton
Production - Natausha Greenblott
Creative Director - Michael Leon
Publisher - Karla Olson

**ENVIRONMENTAL BENEFITS STATEMENT**

**Patagonia Inc** saved the following resources by printing the pages of this book on chlorine free paper made with 100% post-consumer waste.

| TREES | WATER | ENERGY | SOLID WASTE | GREENHOUSE GASES |
|---|---|---|---|---|
| 174 | 14,000 | 73 | 600 | 74,800 |
| FULLY GROWN | GALLONS | MILLION BTUs | POUNDS | POUNDS |

Environmental impact estimates were made using the Environmental Paper Network Paper Calculator 4.0. For more information visit www.papercalculator.org

**1%**
**FOR THE PLANET**
MEMBER

**FSC**
www.fsc.org
MIX
Paper from responsible sources
FSC® C016245

FRONT COVER  A repaired and revived down jacket begins its second life. TIM DAVIS

FIRST PAGE  The Fitz Roy skyline, Patagonia, Argentina. CHOONGOK SUNWOO

PAGE 2  Friends gather for Thanksgiving 1974 near Tuttle Creek, high above Owens Valley, California. GARY REGESTER

TITLE PAGE  The jacket on the cover before restoration. TIM DAVIS

This book is dedicated to all Patagonia colleagues—
the soul of the company—past, present, and future.

Contents

Preface 8

1 What Crisis? 14

2 Meaningful Work 24

3 The Elements of Business Responsibility 88

4 What to Do? 122

5 Sharing What You Learn 132

6 Making a Living in the Anthropocene 140

7 What's Next for Patagonia? 164

Appendix: The Checklists 172

Recommended Reading 195

Acknowledgments 196

About the Authors 197

Index 200

The July 2016 premiere of *Unbroken Ground* held behind the Patagonia store in Ventura, California. Patagonia and Chouinard Equipment have called this courtyard home since 1966. The original blacksmith shop is behind the screen. Other buildings in the background are the Child Development Center and administrative offices. KYLE SPARKS

# Preface

In the decade since we wrote *The Responsible Company: What We've Learned from Patagonia's First 40 Years*, dramatic shifts have taken place in the world and at Patagonia. This new edition, which marks our fiftieth year in business, reflects these changes. The aim of the book, however, remains the same: to articulate the elements of business responsibility for our time—when everyone working at every level has to face the unintended consequences of a 250-year-old industrial model that can no longer be sustained ecologically, socially, or financially.

Yvon has said that Patagonia—or any company for that matter—should behave as though it will be around in 100 years. You don't pump up and hollow out a company meant to stay in business for a good long time. This once-standard American business ethos was eclipsed in the 1960s by Milton Friedman's doctrine of shareholder primacy, wherein the sole purpose of a business is to maximize profits. That objective helps keep a stock's price high but doesn't work in the long run for society, the planet, or even the health of a business. In the 1950s, the average corporation survived to celebrate its sixty-first birthday; now it barely makes it to twenty.

Business founders don't live forever. And a fifty-year-old company that wants to live responsibly for another fifty years needs a succession plan that involves far more than a change of the person sitting at the head of the table. In 2012, Patagonia became a California benefit corporation, which allowed us to enshrine into our business charter our core values and practices, including an annual gift of 1 percent of sales to grassroots environmental organizations. The company's longtime purpose statement—"Build the best product, cause no unnecessary harm, and use business to inspire and implement solutions to the environmental crisis"—could now legally outlast our original ownership. To dissuade anyone of different values from buying in, we required a vote of 100 percent of the company shares to alter the charter.

8

Solving a puzzle in the Forge, the home of Patagonia's advanced R & D team, Ventura, California. TIM DAVIS

Dismayed by the deepening crisis, and the ineffective response from businesses and governments, Yvon rewrote our statement in 2018 to reflect a sharper focus: "We're in business to save our home planet."

It had been nearly thirty years since Patagonia first committed to "inspire and implement solutions," thirty years of effort to "cause no unnecessary harm." We were proud of our work and the products that resulted, but whatever we did each day to push the rock uphill, it came tumbling back down. Global economic activity trespassed ever more of the planet's physical boundaries: Greenhouse gases climbed, storms intensified, rivers dried at the mouth, soil turned to dust, and species continued to disappear at a thousand times their natural rate.

Our sharpened purpose, though, meant more than a race against the doomsday clock. We'd learned something new and promising over the last decade from Patagonia Provisions, our venture into the food business. Regenerative organic practices to cultivate food and fiber could restore topsoil, slow the depletion of groundwater and pollution of rivers, draw carbon from the atmosphere deep into the soil, restore habitat, improve biodiversity, and along the way, help revive the health of rural communities.

In 2016, we introduced organic Long Root Ale made with Kernza, a perennial wheatgrass with roots that descend ten feet or deeper, where they create the proper conditions for microbes and fungi to generate topsoil. Two years later, we began working with smallholder farmers in India to grow organic cotton with regenerative practices, including companion planting of turmeric to discourage harmful insects and generate a second source of income.

Patagonia Provisions pointed our apparel business toward a new North Star. We could do better than doing less harm or becoming carbon neutral. We could give back to Earth as much as or more than we take. We could do positive good.

In 2022, the Chouinard family committed the entire value of the company—monetary and moral—to our new purpose. The family donated 100 percent of the company's stock to two entities—an irrevocable Patagonia Purpose Trust and a 501 (c) (4) charitable organization, the Holdfast Collective, that commits Patagonia's annual profits to groups working to save our home planet. Earth is now our sole shareholder.

I remember being ushered, a few years back, into the office of a dean of a small liberal arts college after giving a talk there. The dean, a pale man in his sixties wearing a gray suit and tie, was responsible for helping graduates find their first real jobs. He had a serious problem, he said, lowering his voice to an anguished whisper: "None of them will go to work for bad companies."

That's a good problem to have. If the elements of business responsibility have not changed much in the past decade, their cultural context certainly has. Young people now want to work for responsible companies; business students know there is no longer a convincing financial case to be made for being a bad company.

Drawing on our experience at Patagonia (the only company we know in any depth), we hope to write usefully for all people who see the need for deep change in business practices and who may work in companies quite unlike ours. Although we mainly address companies that make things, or, like us, design things made by others, this book is germane to all businesses, as well as civic organizations and nonprofits, that want to treat their people well and improve the environmental performance of their operations. Although of particular interest to business leaders and managers, this book is for anyone who wants to engage their best, deepest self in the working life that stretches ahead.

– *Vincent Stanley with Yvon Chouinard*

# 1
# What Crisis?

Wilderness is, in the words of naturalist Margaret Murie, where the hand of man does not linger. It is as much a spiritual concept as a definition of place. Humans are part of nature, and if we had no experience of it in its wild state, we would lose entirely our sense of human scale. We need to engage with the magnificence and mystery of the unknown to know ourselves and our place in the world. Emerson, Thoreau, and other transcendentalists learned and taught these lessons in New England in the 1830s through the 1860s. We can learn, they said, directly from nature about who we are and how to live.

Theodore Roosevelt agreed. After a transformative camping trip to Yosemite in 1903, where he skipped the comfort of a cabin to sleep in a bedroll under the stars, the president became committed to preserving American wilderness. Before leaving office, he would designate 230 million acres as protected public land.

It might surprise some to know that, in 1972, Roosevelt's political descendant Richard Nixon, who a year later would sign the Endangered Species Act, wrote:

> *This is the environmental awakening. It marks a new sensitivity of the American spirit and a new maturity of American public life. It is working a revolution in values, as commitment to responsible partnership with nature replaces cavalier assumptions that we can play God with our surroundings and survive. It is leading to broad reforms in action, as individuals, corporations, government, and civic groups mobilize*

In August 2021, high winds drove the Caldor Fire through the Eldorado National Forest near Pollock Pines, California. MAX WHITTAKER *to conserve resources, to control pollution, to anticipate and prevent emerging environmental problems, to manage the land more wisely, and to preserve wildness.*

Fifty years after Nixon wrote that, Americans are the most avid practitioners of the high-growth, material-intensive capitalism that is to blame for nature's destruction. If the United States is the birthplace of conservation, of the very idea of wilderness as its own value and of nature as a teacher, its citizens have behaved more as conquerors than stewards of the wild.

*We harm nature by what we add to it.*

One example from our watch: perfluorinated compounds (PFCs) that the outdoor industry, including Patagonia (before phasing them out), has used as effective, durable repellents against water and dirt. Known as "forever chemicals," PFCs are toxic and don't break down and dissolve when they enter waterways, the stomachs of birds, or the human bloodstream. For the past 200 years, industry has created a colossal number of chemicals, in massive amounts, that living things previously didn't have to absorb. The Environmental Protection Agency (EPA) identified 62,000 industrial chemicals in 1982, without screening or proscribing their use. Another 24,000 or so have been added since then. Only a few hundred have been tested. Only nine have been banned. You carry in your body, in addition to PFCs, traces of 200 chemicals unknown to your ancestors, some of them toxic in large amounts, others slow-acting carcinogens in small amounts. A chemical present in your blood may have no effect on its own but prove dangerous in combination with another. Untested interactions among the various chemicals released into nature can form up to three billion combinations.

Because we know so little, it is difficult to trace our diseases back to their environmental source. Certain diseases have become prevalent in affluent countries at much higher rates than in the less developed world, which may reflect reduced physical resilience. These include inflammatory autoimmune disorders like asthma, allergies, lupus, and multiple sclerosis. Nonsmokers who reach middle age can now expect to have levels of chronic obstructive pulmonary disease (COPD), a precursor to emphysema, equal to that of smokers. Breast cancer rates for women have tripled during the past forty years, and only 5 to 10 percent of breast cancers are considered hereditary.

Scientists are slow to link specific cancers to specific environmental causes, such as high-voltage wires, polychlorinated biphenyls (PCBs) in the river, or your cell phone. Few cancer catalysts have been studied as closely or confirmed as definitively as cigarette smoke. But some environmentally caused illnesses can be clearly traced: We know that mercury poisoning results from eating too many large predatory fish, such as tuna and swordfish.

Through runoff from sewage and fertilizer, we have added significantly to the nitrogen and phosphorus in the water supply. These extra nutrients create algae blooms that choke off oxygen and kill fish. Half the lakes in Asia, Europe, and North America suffer from such eutrophication, as does much of the Gulf of Mexico.

*We harm nature by altering it.*

The atmospheric concentration of carbon dioxide has now reached its highest level in four million years and continues to grow, making hot air hotter, cold air colder, and increasing the ferocity of storms. Arctic winter ice decreased 9 percent each decade for three decades; in the past decade, it decreased 13 percent, and every winter, more of western Antarctica's ice shelves calve into the ocean.

*We have borrowed from nature what we can't pay back.*

In 1960, humanity consumed about half of the planet's potential resource capacity. By 1987, we exceeded it. Twenty-five years later we were using the resource capacity of one and a half planets. Now we are using the resource capacity of one and three-quarters planets.

The pattern of consumption is lopsided. Europe, proportionate to its population, consumes the equivalent resources of three planets; for North America, the number is seven. Meanwhile, China and India, the world's most populous countries, now have sizable, growing, and resource-consuming middle classes.

Alfred North Whitehead described the "perpetual novelty" we experience from nature's "creative advance." But nature generates its changes at a much slower pace than we now allow and in more complex ways than we can easily recognize. As a result, we're now in the midst of the planet's sixth extinction crisis (the fifth was that of the dinosaurs). In a 2009 article in *Nature*, Johan Rockström identified nine "Earth-system processes and associated thresholds, which, if crossed, could generate unacceptable environmental change." Biodiversity is the "planetary boundary" humans have violated most.

The threshold for an extinction crisis is a loss of ten species per million per year. We are losing species now at the rate of 100 per million per year, or 1,000 times (not a typo) the normal rate. Among the most imminently vulnerable are 30 percent of amphibians and 21 percent of mammals, including the polar bear, rhinoceros, tiger, giraffe, and gorilla. Meanwhile, 12 percent of bird species are threatened with extinction, as are 73 percent of flowering plants, 27 percent of corals, and 50 percent of fungi and protists.

None of this matters if you can persuade one of the Silicon Valley billionaires to let you accompany them to a new life on Mars. We understand that among those who remain on Earth, not everyone suffers from the loss of the polar bear on its melting ice floe or the rhino gone from its muddy African river. But biodiversity, critical in its own right, is also key to human survival—biological and economic. More than half of the global gross domestic product (GDP), the standard—if deeply flawed—measure of the world's aggregated economic output, depends on the capacity of nature to deliver "ecosystem services." If the rain doesn't fall, grass doesn't grow. As bees fail to thrive, so do the

An earlier-than-normal ice-out begins near Spitsbergen, Svalbard, Norway.  HEIKE ODERMATT / MINDEN PICTURES

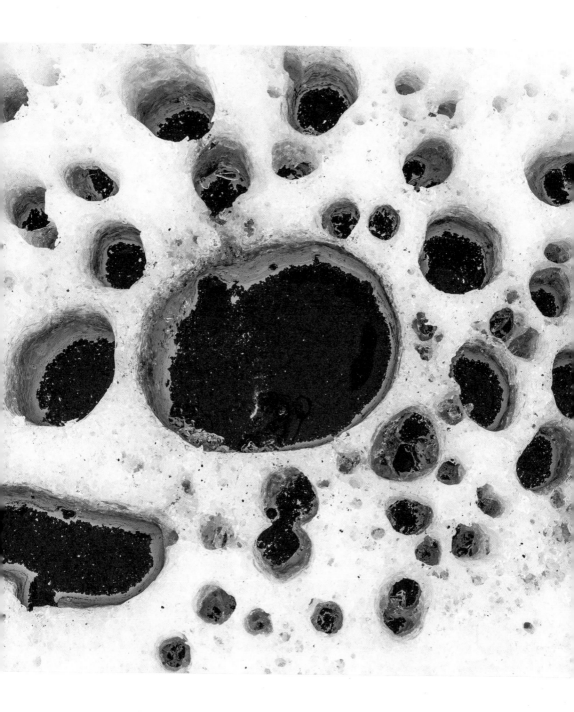

In 2014, during an experimental pulse flow of dammed water, the Colorado River flows into the Sea of Cortez for the first time in decades and revives dormant wetlands. PETER MCBRIDE

plants they no longer pollinate. Fish cannot live in water deprived of oxygen by chemical runoff from farmland.

And fish cannot live where there is no water at all. Withdrawals from lakes and rivers have doubled since 1960. As more of the Earth's major rivers—on which huge populations depend—fail to reach the sea, the ocean's coastal eutrophic, or dead, zones expand. The dammed Colorado River now rarely flows into the Gulf of California, and its former delta is a toxic swamp. Very shortly, no major Chinese river will meet the ocean all year long, which will devastate wetlands and the birds and fish that rely on them.

Worldwide, wetlands diminish and disappear every year, as do coral reefs and mangroves; major fisheries are collapsing. Loss of rainforest continues in poorer countries and in not-so-poor Brazil. Conventional plowing and planting without crop rotation has led to significant loss of topsoil—at the rate of one inch per year in the American Midwest. It takes 500 years for two millimeters of topsoil to form naturally.

The consequences of human overreach are magnified in poor and/ or overpopulated countries. Shrinking resources only aggravate the long-standing challenges of inadequate food, water, and sanitation.

In short, the world is turning into desert. Globalization, a human-made but not humanly controlled process, is largely responsible for the current speed at which life turns to sand. Globalization moves with great speed to identify, then harvest resources for human needs, but crawls slowly to repair the devastation left in its wake. It is fast but stupid, brutal, and imprecise; to cull a tree, it takes out a forest. The richer the country, the greater the waste.

Those who watch the forest being cut and raise their voices against it cannot be heard when the company that cuts the trees does not belong to the community. When local politics becomes subservient to distant economic power, the concept of citizenship, of its duties and possibilities, loses its meaning. The human commons loses its value; it, too, becomes desert.

Democracy is often a condition of ecological health. In 2022, the Environmental Performance Index (EPI) ranked the world's ten top countries as Denmark, the United Kingdom, Finland, Malta, Sweden, Luxembourg, Slovenia, Austria, Switzerland, and Iceland. Most of these countries have small populations, but other European nations, including the Netherlands, Germany, France, and Norway, regularly make the top twenty. No autocracies do. Citizens with no power to act will not be able to save the planet or defend its ability to heal itself.

Yet over the past decade, the world—capitalist or communist, democratic or autocratic—has in critical ways agreed to what needs to be done to halt the desert's spread and restore ecological health. In 2015, more than 180 nations signed on to the Paris Accords, which led to the Science Based Targets initiative to achieve a net-zero world by 2050. A later US withdrawal was mercifully temporary.

Also in 2015, the world's nations agreed to the seventeen UN Sustainable Development Goals (SDGs), which created a crucial common language and specific courses of action for businesses, governments, and civil society to achieve by 2050. The SDGs implicitly acknowledged what Pope Francis described in his encyclical *Laudato Si': On Care for Our Common Home* as one crisis with two faces, social and environmental; they called on countries, rich and poor, to develop economies in support of ecological and social health. Multinational businesses could retire their endless committee discussions about what a company should do to be a good global citizen and instead get to work.

That work is now behind schedule on all fronts, greenwashing is rampant, and there is a lot of what Greta Thunberg calls "blah, blah, blah." But the agreement in its tattered state stands. Powering industry (and homes) through renewable energy is no longer an economic challenge; prices have fallen by 90 percent over the decade. There is no denying the big carbon culprits: cars and other forms of transportation, cows, cement, fertilizer. Businesspeople and politicians have committed to greening the economy for practical as well as cynical reasons.

Greening means, in certain sectors, simply slowing the economy. During the early days of the COVID-19 pandemic, few could ignore that the decline of economic activity quickly reduced levels of pollution, including emissions of greenhouse gases. The world of plants and animals quickened its pulse and showed signs of thriving. We saw that nature wants to come back, that changing our behavior really does matter.

In 2021, the Biden administration embraced a worldwide initiative called 30×30, which calls for the conservation of 30 percent of the globe's marine and terrestrial habitat by 2030. The biologist E. O. Wilson went further, though on a longer timescale, calling for a Half-Earth approach to preserve 50 percent of the Earth's land and oceans by 2050. We strongly support that. As of 2022, only 17 percent of the Earth's land and 8 percent of its oceans are protected. We all depend on the whole web of life: biodiversity. It would be cold irony, indeed, if humanity were to find a way to live with fewer cars and cows, electrify the economy, and finesse climate change but still suffer extinction because we paid so little attention to the conditions of health for forms of life other than our own.

# 2

# Meaningful Work

Everyone wants to have meaningful work, but what exactly makes work meaningful? And what does meaningful work have to do with the responsible company?

At its heart, to have meaningful work is to do something for a living that you love and are good at doing. Most people don't know, at first, what they love best. What they become best at develops by trial and error or by accident. We're all good at something: with words or numbers, or working with our hands, or working outside.

One of the authors of this book, Yvon, would rather spend his day picking apricots or working in his garden than sit at a desk and stare into a computer screen. Repetitive, rhythmic work need not be numbing, as anyone who has spent all day hammering pitons at the forge knows: It can be enlightening. Or joyous, as in the scene in *Anna Karenina* where the aristocrat Levin scythes wheat with his peasants: He can't keep up with them until he learns how to fall into the rhythm. Vincent, on the other hand, once spent a muddy October picking grapes for a living and has to be prodded to work outside in the garden. He doesn't mind the screen, although he prefers pen and paper.

No responsible company can function well without a lot of different people doing things they love to do in concert with one another. At Patagonia we have found that doing what you love—but also doing the right thing—with others is what makes work meaningful.

Although this book is not a history of Patagonia, this chapter draws on our experience to show how one company's responsible actions (some small, some large) help make work meaningful for its

Yvon Chouinard at the grinder on a mild day in the Chouinard
Equipment courtyard, Ventura, California, circa 1970. TOM FROST

employees; and how responsible behavior, as it becomes cumulative, makes a company smarter, nimbler, and potentially more successful.

+++

In their early days, Chouinard Equipment for Alpinists and Patagonia attracted the disaffected, people who loved climbing and surfing or vagabonding best, and would come back to Ventura to pick up work for a few months at a time. Or people who had a degree in physics or biology but for one reason or another, usually the inability or unwillingness to fit into an academic culture, changed course. They would find a home at Patagonia, in a culture congenially filled with other outsiders—the way Paris and Manhattan were for twentieth-century artists.

A high school guidance counselor told Kristine Tompkins's mother not to waste her money sending her daughter to college. Kris, an unmotivated and indifferent student, would by age thirty become Patagonia's CEO during its critical early days. (In midlife, with her husband Doug Tompkins, Kris would help save or restore more than two million acres of exhausted ranchland and surrounding wilderness in Chile and Argentina.) We did not bristle with overachievers who could find reward in what we all saw as the real world. Instead, we attracted bright, restless, unconventional people like Kris who hadn't felt the call toward a vocation, and others who had sought and then abandoned one, or had pursued one that couldn't provide a living.

Many Patagonia employees turned out to have a vocation working for a small, quirky company where no one knew what they couldn't do, so they ended up doing things, with the help of coworkers, they had no idea they could do. Something as ostensibly silly as working in the clothing business turned out to engage the intelligence, imagination, and social needs of our unconventional, antiestablishment colleagues.

Today, Patagonia employs a lot of people who found their vocation early and answered it. They were drawn to color from infancy

Chouinard Equipment's venture into the rag trade sparks joy: Julio Varela, Hall Stratton, and Gary Kennedy attempt a fashion shoot in front of the original retail store in Ventura, circa 1972. CHOUINARD COLLECTION

An injured red-tailed hawk keeps an eye on Kim Stroud, then-manager of our sample sewing shop. Kim, Malinda Chouinard, and Wayne Skankey started a raptor rehabilitation facility at Patagonia that cared for the injured birds. The Ojai Raptor Center is still operating under Kim's lead. TIM DAVIS

or started sewing clothes of their own design when they were ten or earned a graduate degree in textile chemistry. We have MBAs who really love business for itself and others who earned the degree to help them do well in life. (We're not awash in entrepreneurs who would rather be working for themselves.)

Patagonia also has bright locals who grew up in the Ventura area, feel at home here, don't want to leave, and find our company the most interesting place in town to work. It's the best place in town for women to work. Conversely, we have a few top executives who don't want to live in Ventura because their families are settled elsewhere; they can afford to commute and do.

As was true for other companies, our campus felt abandoned during the COVID pandemic, every desk left as it was the night before we shut down for two years. Many employees left town to be closer to the mountains or to grandparents who could help those working from home with children.

Many people seek work at Patagonia because the company's values reflect their own. That deep sympathy provides the extra motivation it takes to stay levelheaded and alert when a workday gets difficult. It keeps people engaged when they have to work hard to find a new fabric source because the old one contains a toxic dye, or negotiate with a factory to invest a jaw-dropping sum in better ventilation, or persuade a realtor that raw farmland is not where Patagonia should place a new distribution center. Doing the right thing motivates us to work past the point where we might otherwise give up. Meaningful work, it turns out, is not only doing what we love but also giving back to the world. The combination creates the ground for a kind of excellence ordinary humans can and want to achieve.

If it wants to become more responsive and responsible, a company needs to cultivate this ordinary human excellence. Every time people in the company do something new that was formerly thought impossible, they contribute significantly to the company's culture, and to the sense that much will be possible in the future. We can think of several critical moments in Patagonia's past that changed our sense of the possible, when we became a more responsible and thus more motivated company without necessarily knowing we were doing so (we were just trying to sell some clothes for a living).

What follows are some of the moments and people who increased our sense of responsibility and our capacity to act responsibly. We'd like to show how these moments built on one another. The intention here is less to celebrate our own experience than to tell some stories you might find reassuring and instructive, and helpful in the course of your own work. We'd like to show how any group of people going about their business can come to realize their environmental and social responsibilities, and then begin to act on them; and how their realization is progressive. One action builds on the one before.

Some background first:

You should know that at its beginning, Patagonia was meant to be an easy-to-milk cash cow, not a risk-taking, environment-obsessed, navel-gazing company. Yvon created Patagonia as an offshoot of Chouinard Equipment for Alpinists, which made excellent mountain-climbing gear that was recognized as the best in the world but generated very little money. Patagonia was intended to be a clean and easy company—desk jockey's work—in contrast to the ten hours a day of sweat and toil needed to hammer out pitons in a coal-fired forge or drill and cut chocks from extruded aluminum. The clothing business required no expensive dies to amortize and had a much broader customer base than a few dirtbag climbers. Who knew then that cotton could be as filthy as coal?

Our responsibilities as businesspeople came slowly and almost involuntarily to light as we focused on the "real" work of designing, making, and selling our clothes. We did not set out to be a responsible company, but time after time, we stumbled into virtue after discovering we were causing harm. In the stories that follow, we'll describe a handful of

General manager Roger McDivitt and national accounts manager
Cindy Nichols double as models for the new polypropylene underwear, circa 1975. PATAGONIA ARCHIVES

moments that stunned us into consciousness (including the discovery that cotton, what we thought was a natural and therefore virtuous fiber, turned out to be the most toxic) to illustrate how one step makes the next, often more complex, step possible—a simple but key lesson.

At Chouinard Equipment, we were used to a life-or-death standard of product quality: You did not sell an ice ax without checking it closely for a hairline fracture or any other fault. Although we applied the same standard to rugby shirts (they had to be thick and tough to survive the skin-shredding sport of rock climbing), we knew that seam failure was unlikely to kill anyone. At the beginning, Patagonia was to be our *irresponsible* company, bringing in easy money, a softer life, and enough profits to keep the climbing business in the black.

We used to think we were somehow exceptional as a business: Patagonia grew out of a small band of climbers and surfers who had a love for the natural world, with a palpable need to be in it and feel a part of it. Thirty years ago, we didn't think we had much to say to the man or woman next to us on the plane wearing "business clothes." Now, though, the businessperson on the plane is more likely to be wearing Patagonia than a suit; and we can think of several topics we might have discussed, from design to inventory control to the impact of material shortages on the balance sheet. We now know that Patagonia is exceptional only at the margins. As mice and men share 99 percent of their genes, so do Amazon, Exxon, Twitter ... and Patagonia.

That 1 percent difference, though, has been significant throughout the past half century and will become more so in the next. As climbers and surfers, our direct engagement with nature allowed us to recognize the environmental crisis earlier than others. And because Patagonia was privately held, we were able to take on greater risks to fight it. When we were successful, others more constrained by convention would follow suit.

While people in the cities and suburbs of the United States, Europe, and Japan experienced an improvement in local air and water quality over the past five decades, those who ventured into wild places saw something different: for climbers, the melting of glaciers; for anglers, the decline in wild fish stocks (in number and size) and a growth in oxygen-reducing algae blooms from agricultural runoff; for surfers and skin divers, the decline at the ocean's edge—the loss of mangroves, coral, and life in the tide pools.

Others, too, took note: Scientists saw the speed with which species were going extinct, and the cumulative effects on the water and atmosphere of chemicals whose half-life exceeded that of any known civilization. City planners saw underground aquifers that stored water for millennia going dry. Independent commercial fishermen, competing with giant trawlers, had to travel farther offshore to make their living. Farmers struggled to adapt to the diminishing thickness of their topsoil (the result of applying expensive chemical fertilizers and pesticides year after year) and to the warming climate that challenged everything they and their forebears had come to know about their land.

The experience and love of the wild defined the small but significant difference between Patagonia and, for example, an Exxon. Something changes when you get a mile from the road into the mountains or forest or paddle out from shore to face the power of the wind and waves. The elemental world, where human systems do not protect us, is humbling; at the same time, it allows us to feel more self-reliant. We become aware of the wild beyond us but also of the wild within.

At Patagonia, our experiences in the wild helped us understand the vital connection between wilderness and the towns and cities where most of us lived: For us, it was clear that the health of nature undergirds the health of our social and industrial systems.

## Climbing Clean

In 1972, Chouinard Equipment for Alpinists was still a small company (about $400,000 a year in sales), but it had become the largest supplier

Sean Villanueva O'Driscoll places protection for the second pitch of Frame by Frame, on Poll an Iomair, a limestone sea cliff, Inis Mór, Aran Islands, Ireland.  SAM BIÉ

of climbing hardware in the United States. With the increased popularity of climbing, and its concentration on the same well-tried routes (in Yosemite Valley, Eldorado Canyon, the Shawangunks, etc.), our reusable hard-steel pitons had become environmental villains. The same fragile cracks had to endure repeated hammering of pitons during both placement and removal, and the disfiguring was severe. After an ascent of the degraded Nose route on El Capitan, which had been pristine a few summers earlier, Yvon and partner Tom Frost decided to phase out of the piton business. It was a huge risk because pitons were the mainstay of the business. But the change had to be made for reasons both moral and practical: The routes were beautiful and satisfying and shouldn't be ruined; and to ruin them would put an end to, or greatly reduce, the possibilities for climbing in the most popular areas, and thus eventually hurt our business.

There was an alternative: aluminum chocks that could be wedged in and removed by hand without the use of a hammer. Hexentrics and Stoppers made their first appearance in the 1972 catalog.

That catalog opened with an editorial from the owners on the environmental hazards of pitons. A fourteen-page essay by Sierra climber Doug Robinson on how to use chocks began with a powerful paragraph:

> *There is a word for it, and the word is clean. Climbing with only nuts and runners for protection is clean climbing. Clean because the rock is left unaltered by the passing climber. Clean because nothing is hammered into the rock and then hammered back out, leaving the rock scarred and the next climber's experience less natural. Clean because the climber's protection leaves little trace of his ascension. Clean is climbing the rock without changing it; a step closer to organic climbing for the natural man.*

Within a few months of the catalog's mailing, the piton business had atrophied; chocks sold faster than we could make them. In the tin sheds of Chouinard Equipment, the steady pounding rhythm of the drop hammer gave way to the high-pitched whine of the multiple-drill jig.

We learned that we could inspire our customers to do less harm simply by making them aware of the problem and offering a solution. We also learned that by addressing the problem, we had forced ourselves to make a better product: Chocks were lighter than pitons and as secure or more so. We would not have risked the obsolescence of our piton business just to sell something new. But doing the right thing motivated us—and turned out to be good business.

Befriending the Ventura River

If you took a train from France to Italy around the time Chouinard Equipment for Alpinists started making chocks, you might have noticed the Italians in your compartment tossing their lunch wrappers, crumpled cigarette packs, and wine bottles cheerfully out the window into the countryside until the train crossed the border into Italy, at which time the same people would turn fastidious and toss their garbage in the waste bin. One did not trash the mother country.

At Chouinard Equipment, we were the opposite. We cared much about the mountains but not much about Ventura, a funky little oil patch and lemon-packing town with a lot of junk shops, hazardous waste, and a dead river. Nature was something you drove to.

In our travels during the 1960s and '70s, we saw what was happening in the remote corners of the world: creeping pollution and deforestation, the slow, then not-so-slow, disappearance of fish and wildlife. And we saw what was happening closer to home: thousand-year-old sequoias succumbing to LA smog, the thinning of life in tide pools and kelp beds, the rampant development of the land along the coast. But we did not see what was happening at home.

By the 1980s, we'd begun to read about global warming, the cutting and burning of tropical forests, the rapid loss of groundwater and topsoil, acid rain, the ruin of rivers and creeks from silting-over dams. The descriptions we read of environmental destruction reinforced what we'd seen with our own eyes and smelled with our own noses on our journeys. Slowly, we became aware that uphill environmental battles fought by small, dedicated groups of people to save patches of land and stretches of water could yield significant results.

Around that time, a group of us went to a city council meeting to help protect the California Street surf break. We knew vaguely that the Ventura River had once been a major steelhead salmon habitat. During the forties, two dams had been built, and water diverted. Except for winter rains, the only water left at the river mouth flowed from the sewage plant. At the city council meeting, several experts testified that the river was dead and that channeling the mouth would have no effect on remaining bird- and wildlife, or on our surf break.

Then Mark Capelli, a shy-seeming twenty-five-year-old biology student, gave a slide show of photos he had taken along the river—of the birds that lived in the willows, of the muskrats and water snakes, of eels that spawned in the estuary. When he showed a slide of a steelhead smolt, everyone stood up to cheer. Yes, fifty or so steelhead still came to spawn in our "dead" river.

The development plan was defeated. Patagonia gave Mark a desk, a phone, a mailbox, and small contributions to help him fight the river's battle. As more development plans cropped up, the Friends of the Ventura River worked to defeat them, and to clean up the water and increase its flow. Wildlife increased, and more steelhead returned to spawn.

Mark taught us three important lessons: A grassroots effort could make a difference; a degraded habitat could, with effort, be restored; and the natural world wasn't just in the faraway silent places. Nature still lived outside wilderness, even in our funky oil and ag town, and we could help give it some space to thrive. We had a responsibility to do so.

## Kids

During the early seventies, one of the co-owners of Chouinard
Equipment for Alpinists, Dorene Frost, used to bring her daughter,
Marna, to work; no one minded. After the Chouinards' son, Fletcher,
was born, Malinda brought him in; then as other workers had babies,
they brought them in as well. You could find baby blankets draped
over computer monitors, and rattles and toy trains littered the floor.
And, of course, kids cried.

The noise prompted a discussion about providing babysitting
on-site, not as a progressive measure—childcare in the workplace in
those days was so rare we didn't even know it was progressive. The
mothers who worked for us simply wanted to be near their babies, to
breastfeed or comfort them when needed.

The men at the company, including this book's authors, and the
women without kids, including the CEO, didn't think Patagonia
should devote its scarce cash or space to running a "nursery school."
But, backed by the mothers, Malinda doggedly pursued her cause and
eventually won. The kids stayed, and they have made a difference to
the quality of our workday.

First, the sight and sound of children playing in their yard makes
the place feel more human and less corporate. The presence of children makes adults conscious of their responsibilities as mammals:
adult human beings, first; employees, second. It is hard to be officious
around a four-year-old. And it is a balm for parents to have their
children nearby. Our high-quality childcare, maternal and paternal
leave, and flextime policies have lifted some of the barriers that block
working mothers from advancement. When we require a new, often-
nursing mother to travel for work, for instance, she is accompanied
by a provider from our Child Development Center, at our expense.
The program helps families advance in unexpected ways: Our wetsuit
repair specialist, Hector Castro, brought his daughter with him

Fletcher, Malinda, and Yvon Chouinard in the "shop,"
1977. The Chouinards are wearing two of Patagonia's
original styles: Malinda, a Sailor Shirt; Yvon, a Chamonix
Guide Sweater. CHOUINARD COLLECTION

Thinking inside the box at Patagonia's childcare center.
KYLE SPARKS

to Patagonia while his wife attended school during the day. "If we were strapped financially because of day care," he says, "we probably wouldn't be making these leaps and setting these goals."

The kids, a cohort that began officially in 1983, grow up to be wonderful adults—we're as proud of that as we are of the clothes we produce.

Providing on-site childcare turned out to be a good business decision. We have a very low employee turnover rate, especially among parents of school-age children. The presence of kids and the introduction of childcare taught us that if there is some quality about the workplace you (and your employees) love and don't want to lose, then don't.

We charge tuition but subsidize the childcare programs heavily in Ventura and at our distribution center in Reno. A closer look at the numbers reveals that childcare either contributes to the company's bottom line or costs us pocket change, depending on the metrics used. From the subsidy we subtract our tax credit and savings from employee retention, reduced turnover, and increased employee engagement.

Being one of the first companies in the United States to have on-site childcare set us on a path to initiate rather than follow change. We began to feel more at ease doing things to improve working conditions that most companies avoided, like flextime and job sharing.

## Environmental Giving

Once Mark Capelli taught us what could be done for a degraded local landscape, we knew that beloved patches of land and stretches of water all over the country could be saved or restored. Lots of small groups, with much passion and no money, had begun to work on behalf of the places they loved.

If a mailbox and a bit of cash could make a difference for Mark, so could small grants for others trying to save or restore habitat.

Rounding out the day at the 2015 Patagonia Tools Conference, Stanford Sierra Camp, Fallen Leaf Lake, California. AMY KUMLER

Patagonia began to make regular donations of $1,000 here and $5,000 there. We favored the little groups no other corporation would touch, rather than nongovernmental organizations (NGOs) with big staffs, high overheads, and corporate connections.

In 1985, the company committed to donate 10 percent of profits annually to these groups. We did so for two reasons. First, we wanted to help. Second, we believed we owed the Earth a tax for the industrial impact of our business activities. We consider our giving a cost of doing business, not charity. A year later, we upped the ante to an annual 1 percent of sales: What we do affects the planet whether or not we make a profit.

Craig Mathews, founder of the venerable Yellowstone angler's shop, Blue Ribbon Flies, was another early business donor to environmental causes. In 2002, Craig teamed up with Yvon to create 1% for the Planet, an alliance of companies that pledge 1 percent or more of their annual sales to environmental causes. Now, 1% for the Planet has more than 5,400 members in sixty countries who give to more than 4,000 nonprofits—$435 million as of 2023.

Every two years, Patagonia hosts a "Tools for Grassroots Activists" conference for selected participants from the groups we work with. We bring in experts on core skills (strategy, grassroots organizing, lobbying, fundraising), as well as offer tips on how to work with local business, give a presentation, and use Google Earth technology to bust wrongdoers.

At Patagonia, environmental grant-giving is deeply embedded in the culture. Employees elected by their colleagues to serve on our Grants Council direct the giving each year. They choose the groups and determine the size of each grant. We also run an environmental internship program. Employees apply to work full-time for one of our grantees on a project of their choosing for up to six weeks. Thirty-four employees, twelve stores, and one department took advantage of the program this past year, which amounted to almost 10,000 volunteer hours for forty-three organizations.

## Educating Our Customer

In the spirit of the original Chouinard Equipment clean-climbing catalog, Patagonia undertook—in our own catalogs and, later, on our website—education campaigns to raise the awareness of our customers on environmental topics that had not yet received much general attention. The first environmental essay helped purchase for the Mapuche people of Chile title to their forest, which had been put out to bid for clearcutting. The second supported Julia Butterfly Hill and other tree sitters in their campaign to end clearcutting of Northern California's ancient redwood forests. Most educational campaigns lasted one to three years: We described the need to remove outdated dams that keep fish from reaching their spawning grounds. We alerted people to the deteriorating condition of the oceans and freshwater; and the need for wildlife corridors so animals can migrate through fragmented habitat in a time of climate change.

## Getting Our House in Order

Only after we gained confidence assailing the enemies of nature did we become capable of recognizing the foe in the mirror we had long overlooked. We still had only a partial view of the enemy that was us. By the late 1980s, we could acknowledge that our company of several hundred people engaged directly in activities that polluted the Earth or wasted resources: We flew on planes, printed large runs of catalogs from felled trees, drastically remodeled buildings to house our stores. We did not yet recognize the harm we, ourselves, were doing as a maker of clothes. We were dependent on our supply chain, we thought, and not in a position to convince them to change their ways.

Although we had never been shy about asking our fabric suppliers to make changes that would improve our clothing's performance, we had not yet learned to ask them to use recycled materials, or to

Safe passage for wildlife: An animal overpass near Banff, Alberta, Canada, reconnects vital habitat once separated by asphalt and the flow of cars. JOEL SARTORE

investigate the wastewater policies of the dyehouses that worked with the mills, or to check closely into working conditions on the sewing-factory floor. One early decision, the development and use of recycled polyester, was controversial internally: managers feared the loss of sales because of the low-quality reputation, in that era, of anything called "recycled."

We did slowly gain confidence. We helped develop a quality stock with high postconsumer-recycled content commercially viable for the paper mills. We built new and remodeled old retail-store locations using paints without volatile organic compounds (VOCs), used recycled wood and wallboard, and installed energy-efficient lighting. In 1996, our new distribution center in Reno achieved a 60 percent reduction in energy use through solar-tracking skylights and radiant heating; we used recycled material there for everything from rebar to carpet to urinal partitions. The following year, when we built a three-story office building in Ventura on the former site of Myrt's Cottage Café, we used 95 percent recycled materials.

By 2006, we had the accumulated experience and confidence to successfully seek LEED (Leadership in Energy and Environmental Design) certification for the expansion of our Reno distribution center, even though building to this standard was a first for both our contractor and the Reno area.

By 2018, we had outgrown Reno and sought to reduce emissions from shipping to the entire country from the West Coast. Our operations team hit the road with commercial realtors in search of a site for an East Coast distribution center. As they drove through the rolling hills of Ohio, Tennessee, and Pennsylvania, the realtors waxed rhapsodic about the undeveloped land they showed us. Our operations people were troubled. Why would we pave over acres of farmland or forest to site a 360,000-square-foot warehouse?

With the help of DHL, our distribution partner, we found an alternative, an abandoned mine in Wilkes-Barre, Pennsylvania, that had been reclaimed by the nonprofit Earth Conservancy. The location had a remarkable story. Anthracite coal mining had ended abruptly there sixty years earlier when the Knox Coal Company instructed its miners, illegally, to dig a tunnel too close to the Susquehanna River. As it breached the riverbed walls, the river drowned twelve men and flooded underground coal galleries throughout the region. Most could never be re-entered safely. Among the many local companies ruined was Blue Coal. After decades of bankruptcy proceedings, it took another twenty-two years for Earth Conservancy to stabilize, contour, and revegetate the land that would become home to Patagonia's eastern hub. In this, and other reclamation successes, the Conservancy is fulfilling its long-term goal to restore not only the region's landscape, but its jobs.

We hired Gabby Zawacki, who is from the area, to be our distribution center supervisor. Among her many skills is her ability to decipher the intricate linen maps of the twenty-two levels of coal galleries that still interlace the valley.

Getting our house in order didn't much reduce greenhouse gas emissions generated by the manufacturing and transportation of Patagonia products: As of today, 97 percent of our emissions are generated not by our offices, warehouses, stores, or business travel, but in the supply chain—on farms that grow cotton and in dyehouses, assembly factories, and mills that produce polyester and nylon. Most of that impact comes from the production of the raw materials. Although, for the most part, we no longer use "virgin" synthetics sourced from newly drilled oil, many of the mills that produce our fabrics and the factories that sew our clothing are still powered by coal or other non-renewable energy sources.

We are committed to becoming carbon neutral, which means we must eliminate, capture, or otherwise mitigate the carbon emissions for which we're responsible. To do so, we're working cooperatively with the mills, factories, and farms that supply us and helping them

Employees pay tribute to the tropics in front of the
Patagonia Boston store. A ventilation problem in this
beautifully restored building alerted us to the dangers
of conventional cotton.  PATAGONIA ARCHIVES

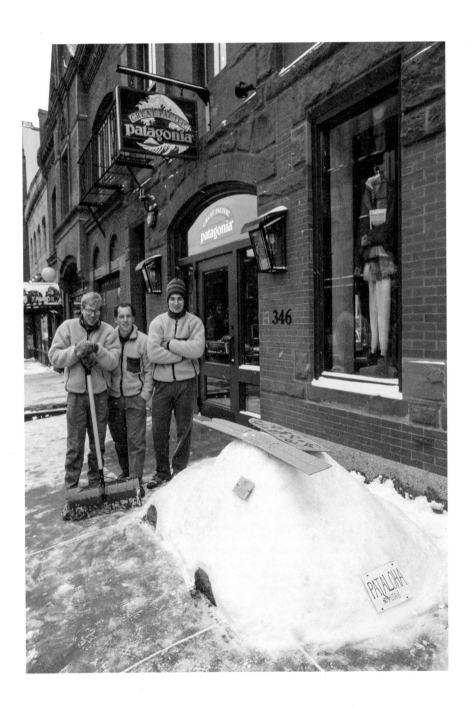

introduce alternative sources of energy. (As of this writing, 82 percent of our environmental impact is in raw materials: Many of the mills we use are still fired by coal.)

## Poisoning Our People

Within days of the 1988 opening of our beautifully restored, then-environmentally state-of-the-art Boston store, our staff began to experience headaches during their shifts. We had the air tested: We learned that the ventilation system was faulty and off-gassing of formaldehyde through the vents was poisoning our staff. A typical business response might have been to fix the ventilation system to make the headaches go away.

The source of the problem turned out to be the finish on our cotton clothes, which was added by the mill to prevent shrinkage and wrinkling. At the time, all we knew about formaldehyde was what we remembered from biology class: the chemical in the jar with the sheep's heart. We discovered that formaldehyde could cause cancer of the nose, nasal cavity, and throat. (The EPA would acknowledge these dangers two decades later when Hurricane Katrina victims got sick from the formaldehyde in their FEMA trailers.) To reduce the use of formaldehyde, yet avoid shrinkage or wrinkling, we learned to use higher-quality long-staple cotton, altered the way the fiber was spun, and preshrank the fabric. Although this added some cost, it was important to us not to sacrifice quality while reducing environmental harm. None of us wanted to have to iron our pants or send them to the dry cleaner to be treated with more chemicals.

It dawned on us that we were failing as a business to lead an examined life. It turned out we didn't know how to make clothing responsibly. What other harms were we causing? We had been conducting our business like any other clothing company. We'd chosen cotton fabrics for their texture and durability, then sent the sample off to a cut-and-sew factory, which would source from a mill, which sourced from a broker, which bundled its raw-cotton purchases, depending on the spot price, from multiple countries. We had no idea where the cotton came from, let alone how it was finished.

So, in 1991, we commissioned a study to assess the environmental impacts of the four fibers most commonly used in our clothes: cotton, polyester, nylon, and wool. It was a shock how badly cotton fared—it turned out to be not much more "natural" than nylon.

It's a horrific story. To prepare soil for planting cotton, workers spray organophosphates (which were developed as nerve gases for World War II and can damage the human central nervous system) to kill all the living organisms. The soil is then doornail dead (five pesticide-free years must pass before earthworms, an indication of soil health, will return). Such soil requires intensive use of artificial fertilizers to hold the cotton plants in place. Rainwater runoff from these fields contributes significantly to the growth of ocean dead zones. Conventional cotton fields, which represent 3 percent of cultivated land, ingest 24 percent of chemical insecticides used in agriculture and 11 percent of pesticides. About one-tenth of 1 percent of these chemicals reach the pests they target.

A conventional cotton field stinks; its chemicals burn the eyes and turn the stomach. Before harvesting in warmer regions like California, cotton is sprayed by a crop duster with the defoliant Paraquat, about half of which hits its target. The rest settles over the neighbors' fields and into our streams.

Genetically modified Bt (*Bacillus thuringiensis*) cotton, introduced in this century, reduces pesticide use initially, especially in temperate climates, by targeting leaf-eating bollworms. China, which planted Bt cotton on a large scale in the early 2000s, found that after a few seasons, grass bugs and other pests immune to Bt stepped into the breach left by the bollworms. Wholesale spraying was resumed. In the United States, bollworms have developed resistance to Bt, so

Monsanto/Bayer, the manufacturer, has adjusted its formula year by year.

Jill Dumain, our chief textile developer, who soon became a toxic chemicals expert, led the search for alternatives. Organic cotton was available from a few family farmers in California and Texas. So, we experimented. At first, we made only T-shirts with organic cotton. Then, after several trips to the conventional cotton fields of the San Joaquin Valley, where we could smell the selenium ponds and see the lunar landscape, we asked ourselves a critical question: How could we continue to make products that laid waste to the Earth this way?

In the fall of 1994, we made the decision to take our cotton sports-wear 100 percent organic by 1996. We had eighteen months to make the switch for sixty-six products, and less than a year to line up the fabric. There simply wasn't enough organic cotton commercially available to buy through brokers, so we went directly to the few farmers who had gone back to organic methods. We talked to the certifiers so that all the fiber could be traced back to the bale. Then we had to go to the ginners and spinners and persuade them to clean their equipment before and after running what for them would be very small quantities. The spinners in particular objected to organic cotton because it was full of leaves and stems and sticky from aphids. Our most creative partner, located in Thailand, solved the problem by freezing the cotton before spinning.

Due to the resourcefulness and open-mindedness of our partners, we succeeded. Every Patagonia garment made of cotton in 1996 was organic and has been ever since. Our cotton odyssey taught us our responsibility for what happens, in Patagonia's name, at every step in the supply chain.

That first fabric assessment also taught us that oil-based polyester could be made less harmful if we used recycled materials rather than those made from oil fresh out of the well. We learned how to make a fleece jacket from twenty-five quart-sized plastic soda bottles melted down and extruded into fiber. Later, we learned that the most efficient way to recycle polyester is to melt down a piece of clothing at the end of its useful life and extrude it into new fiber.

The textile industry is one of the most chemically intensive industries on Earth, second only to agriculture, and the world's largest polluter of increasingly scarce fresh water. The World Bank estimates that about 20 percent of freshwater pollution comes from textile dyeing and finishing. Google Earth satellite images show the Pearl River turns indigo as it flows into the South China Sea, downstream from the world's major jeans factories in Xingtang. Researchers have identified seventy-two toxic chemicals in our water that trace back to textile dyes, which can also compromise the health of millworkers. In addition, the textile industry is a water hog that uses coal- or wood-powered steam to fuel its mills, as well as water-intensive dyeing and finishing processes.

Wastewater that goes—often illegally—untreated or partially treated returns to a river, where it heats the water, increases its pH, and saturates it with dyes, finishes, and fixatives, which in turn leave a residue of salts and metals that leach into farmland or settle into the viscera of fish. As we learned about this in the early 1990s, we scrambled to find factories that recycle their water. During the past decade we have learned to our dismay that pollution also results from cleaning our apparel in home washing machines. All articles of clothing shed microfiber particles—some are not even visible—which make their way into municipal water systems and eventually out to the ocean.

Polyester fleece, including Patagonia's, is a notable culprit because fleece sheds more than more tightly woven constructions and because polyester, as an oil-based fiber, persists in the environment (as do the chemicals used on conventional cotton). Since 2014, we have partnered with the NGO Ocean Wise Plastic Labs and other outdoor brands to develop and recommend solutions to the problem: different fabric construction, better filtration in home washers, changes in municipal water systems. Samsung, the first appliance manufacturer to engage with our efforts, developed a washing machine that captures much of the shedding, and is now at work on a dryer that will do the same. Other manufacturers are following their lead to protect the oceans and rivers from polluted wastewater.

It's important to note that, as with a lot of corporate greening breakthroughs, the shed-capturing washing machine resulted from a stumble (mine) that met with goodwill and ingenuity (Samsung's). When I spoke to a couple hundred of Samsung's leaders in 2019, I mentioned that no washing machine existed to solve the shedding problem. "Say, you make washing machines," I blurted out, immediately regretting my lack of diplomacy. Within a year, Samsung had engineered its new technology and partnered with Patagonia and Ocean Wise to test it before bringing it successfully to market.

A last word about organic cotton: It does the planet no positive good. It only eliminates the use of harmful chemicals. Regenerative agricultural practices, although more labor-intensive, generate far less pollution than the usual organic cotton. To rebuild healthy soils, regenerative practices do more than forgo toxic chemicals. They minimize tillage, employ crop rotation and companion planting, and require less fertilizer (even from natural sources) and less water. These practices restore topsoil far faster than nature can on her own. Healthy soil draws carbon out of the air and deep into the soil. Excellent food grows this way—carrots, peaches, and tomatoes with their full taste and nutrients. Cotton and hemp can grow this way, too, in soil that gives back to the planet rather than bleeding it dry.

Bill McKibben made an interesting point years ago when he compared the yields of factory farming and low-input farming. Subsidized factory farming yields more dollars per acre, but a low-input (not necessarily organic) field yields more food. Factory farming requires

An Arvind regenerative organic cotton farm
in India, 2019.  AVANI RAI

industrial simplicity and heavy engineering: a few hundred acres of straight-rowed crops of the same variety harvested by vehicles as expensive as Ferraris, fueled by copious amounts of oil. A farmer with a few acres, however, must know and walk the land, and rely on intimate knowledge to tease out more of its productivity in order to know where one plant thrives in another's shade, where to intercrop plants with roots of different lengths, and whether the earthworms are thriving. One type of farming exhausts the land, the other takes advantage of and takes part in the natural world.

We now partner with more than 2,500 farmers in India and Peru, most of whom work one- or two-acre plots using regenerative organic methods. By the end of the decade, we hope to source regenerative organic cotton and hemp exclusively. Smallholdings allow the farmer to observe the crop, adapt better to changes in the weather, and control insects. Companion planting of cotton with turmeric or chickpeas gives the farmer a second source of income on land that generates a minimum of debt.

Low-input, small-scale farming, more than the factory farm, represents sound business now and in the future. This is counterintuitive for those who grew up in the twentieth century, with its emphasis on streamlining and scalability. But the time has come for those of us in business to understand ourselves as a part of nature and to walk our fields; we need to make our practices less exhaustive and more productively alive, so that the world will be habitable for those who come after us.

## Our Footprint

Our Footprint, originally named the Footprint Chronicles, presents stories on our website to educate customers, NGOs, suppliers, and our own staff about our environmental and social impact. Our transparency—to ourselves as much as to others—has helped us make

The original version of Our Footprint included an assessment for each of the products described. "The Good," "The Bad," and "What We Think" described what we were proud of in the product described, what needed to be changed, and what we propsoed to do next.

ink
ng for ways to recycle

atagonia

the choice to move beyond the status quo and do better. Doing better has made our work more meaningful: We're not just making clothes, we're making long-lasting clothes that do less damage. And, in part through Our Footprint, our work has inspired others.

By 2005, the corporate social responsibility (CSR) report had become customary for most midsized and large (usually publicly traded) companies. The report was used by NGOs, advocacy groups, and journalists as a tool for examining the comparative business practices of corporations, but Patagonia had not yet created one. We drafted an initial CSR in the vague monotone characteristic of environmental- and social-responsibility reporting. These reports tell you how much the company gives to the symphony but not how many square miles it destroys in the Niger Delta.

We wanted to come up with a more transparent and compelling way to report on our activity—or lack of it; we wanted to engage our customers, as well as researchers numbed by CSR rhetoric. So, we developed Our Footprint as an interactive mini-website that, in its first season, traced five Patagonia products geographically from design to fiber (at its point of origin), to weaving or knitting, to dyeing, to sewing, to delivery to our Reno warehouse. For each product we also calculated carbon emissions, energy use, and waste, as well as the distance traveled from origin to warehouse. We posted this information on the product's online selling page as well.

The idea behind Our Footprint was to examine and communicate the full breadth of Patagonia's life and habits as a company. We wanted to account for every person who worked on Patagonia products on farms and in mills, dyehouses, and factories, not just our employees. We had about 500 people on our payroll engaged in design, testing, sales, marketing, and distribution, whereas up to 10,000 people at any given time worked on Patagonia products throughout the supply chain. We wanted to teach ourselves more deeply about our own business. It was time to bring to the surface the unintended harmful consequences of making all Patagonia clothes. Harm done on an industrial scale could be reduced on an industrial scale.

It is important to note that all this work was done by a staff of two. The small size of the department was deliberate: We wanted the reduction of environmental harm to be part of everyone's job. We did not want to create a separate bureaucracy that might clash unproductively with our product-quality or sourcing staff or give that staff a reason to make environmental considerations secondary because someone else would handle them in their stead. We wanted our enviros to be a welcome, well-regarded resource throughout the company. But they also had considerable clout. The enviro team could, if it found environmental or working conditions unsatisfactory, override or delay the sourcing department's decision to do business with a new factory.

We are no longer, as in the days of Chouinard Equipment for Alpinists, a pre–Industrial Revolution workshop built around a courtyard, a kind of village business. Most of the people who assemble our clothes are poor, darker-skinned, and female. They punch a time clock and work at a machine in a long row marked by a number hung from a ceiling. Day after day, they sew clothes for Patagonia, and on days they don't sew for us, they sew for our competitors. What we're willing to pay their employer helps determine their wages.

## What Does Patagonia Owe These Workers?

From farm to mill to factory, wages are low, as they have been since the beginning of the Industrial Revolution. For two centuries, textile mills and sewing factories have provided entry-level jobs for people in transition from agricultural subsistence to an industrial economy. Once wages in a region rise, people find better jobs. The factories pick up and move on to a new, rural region or country where a fresh crop of people can be enticed to leave farms for the promise of regular pay.

When we got into the apparel business fifty years ago, high-quality cotton sportswear production had already moved from the United States to Hong Kong, then still a British colony. (Until the adoption of NAFTA, we were able to source the fabric for and produce our synthetic clothes in the United States.) Over time, the epicenter for sportswear drifted from Hong Kong to the mainland, then to north and inland China, then finally to Vietnam, Thailand, and Bangladesh. When sewing factories first arrived in a rural area, the managers would recruit young women from the region's farms and set them up in barracks. The women would work hard for a few years to earn their dowry, then go home. Meanwhile, a town would grow up around the factory, and the barracks would no longer be needed.

This idea for unified housing and labor originated in the 1830s in the United States. When the first big integrated textile mills were established in Lowell and Lawrence, Massachusetts, local farmers considered factory work beneath them but agreed to send their daughters to the mills. The girls and women had one-year contracts and lived together in boardinghouses, six to a room, twenty-four to a house.

On a visit from England, Charles Dickens praised the mills' working and living conditions, noting pianos in the boardinghouse parlors and a literary magazine written, as the cover boasted, by "factory operatives." By today's standards, though, conditions were cruel: Women worked from seven to seven, windows were shut to ensure high humidity to keep the yarn moist, cotton lint floated through the air and into the lungs, and an extraordinary level of noise sounded from the crudely calibrated looms.

Once the New England towns grew up around their mills, the boardinghouses closed. By the end of the nineteenth century, the factory labor base had shifted from farm girls to immigrant families. Our own family took part in this history: They sold their farm in Québec to emigrate south to Maine to work the looms of the cotton and woolen mills along the Androscoggin River. The system was efficient.

In 1908, Yvon's father, age nine and in the company of his parents and ten siblings, took the train to Lewiston, Maine. The Grand Trunk Railroad Depot stood opposite the Bates Manufacturing Company's hiring hall. Behind the hall lay a sprawl of four-decker wooden tenements known as P'tit Canada. A family could arrive at the station, secure jobs for everyone who could physically work (age six on up), then walk half a block to rent their rooms—all in a day. The French Canadians took work that Americans by then, including girls and women, would rather not do.

Was it meaningful work? Such a term wouldn't have occurred to our immigrant relatives. They were of a generation in transition from meaningful but hardscrabble work bound to the land to a life of low-paid industrial work that required long hours in uncomfortable, if not unsafe, conditions. They were no longer peasants, but industrial foot soldiers with no independent control over most of their waking hours. Their new life met their basic needs for food and shelter, as well as their social needs: Their friends worked alongside them. According to psychologist Abraham Maslow, however, our family members had yet to meet the two highest, most complex require-ments in the hierarchy of human needs: a sense of worth and self-fulfillment. It was Maslow's view that needs must be met in the order of their importance for survival: basics first, self-fulfillment last. We suspect that as our family members advanced their basic needs, they lost hefty measures of self-worth and self-fulfillment. When they left the farm for the mill, they gained a regular income, which made life easier, but as overworked laborers in a deafening workspace, they lost their autonomy, sense of purpose, and connection to nature. Farm life had been harsh, and in bad years dangerous, but not demeaning in this new way.

The mills eventually moved south from New England to the Carolinas, in successful pursuit of cheaper, nonunion labor, and, ultimately, offshore to Asia and South America. The marathon chase to pay people even less than too little can no longer be won by pulling up stakes in one region and moving to another—and, of course, should never have come this far. Millworkers and sewing operators, like all workers, deserve a living wage. They also have the right to have their highest needs met: the need to be treated respectfully, to give the best of themselves, and to feel that what they are doing helps rather than harms society. No work, anywhere, should be meaningless.

It took us, too, a long time to ask ourselves what we owe people who work for others in our supply chain. We had high sewing standards, even for casual sportswear, and exacting standards for technical clothes. To meet quality requirements, our production staff had always been drawn to clean, well-lighted factories that employed experienced sewing operators. We always bargained with our factories over price and terms, but we never chased lowest-cost labor.

Yet when a labor-rights group revealed that Kathie Lee Gifford's clothing line for Walmart was sewn by twelve-year-olds, we wondered whether we were doing anything close to that. When Gifford said she had no idea, we believed her. We knew how little we knew about our own supply chain. What measures did our factories take to prevent or deal with a fire? Did they use needle guards to prevent injuries? How many hours a week did the women sew? We didn't know. Even in good factories, employees can be forced to work long hours, especially when a company like ours reorders a hot-selling item and pressures for early delivery.

In 1999, we accepted an invitation to join a task force created by President Clinton (in response to the Gifford scandal) to end child labor and improve garment-factory conditions worldwide. Out of this task force came the Fair Labor Association (FLA), an independent nonprofit monitoring organization dedicated to fair pay and decent working conditions. The FLA's Workplace Code of Conduct prohibits child labor, forced labor, violence, sexual and psychological harassment, and racial discrimination. It guarantees minimum legal

The Vertical Knits factory, Patagonia's manufacturer of Responsibili-Tee shirts, organic cotton T-shirts, and cotton sweatshirts in Baca, Mexico. The factory includes a water treatment plant and has solar panels.  KERI OBERLY

or prevailing wage, whichever is higher, overtime wages (with limits on the number of overtime hours allowed, a sticky issue), healthy and safe working conditions, and freedom of association to join a union (though independent unions are outlawed in China and Vietnam). Patagonia has its own Code of Conduct that prevents factories from subcontracting work without our permission.

Patagonia doesn't own farms, mills, or factories. Most of our employees have never been any place where Patagonia clothes are produced at any stage. Yet what is done in our name must not remain invisible to us. We are responsible for every worker who helps make our goods and for all that goes into a piece of clothing that bears a Patagonia label.

During the early 2000s, we made the poor choice to expand our factory base in search of lower-cost labor. Soon we were in more factories than we could handle. We no longer knew many of the people with whom we were dealing or what conditions were like on the factory floor. The result was poor product quality, late delivery, expensive rework, long inspection times at our Reno warehouse, customer dissatisfaction, and loss of profit incurred by honoring customer returns.

We then reduced our factory count by a third and bolstered our relationships with our remaining partners; their factories continuously improved quality, including the quality of life on the job for their workers. We placed as much work as possible with factories we admired and with whom we felt a strong kinship, where everyone from the sewing operator to the factory chief cared about the quality of their work and their day.

We made it a policy to have a member of our social/environmental responsibility team visit a new factory to verify conditions before placing an initial order. This team member can break the deal. Our quality director has similar veto power over the sourcing department's decision to take on a new factory. Our clothes are now made in places where the factory floor does not get too hot and there is natural light. Many factories pay better than prevailing wage and provide a healthy subsidized lunch, low-cost childcare, and a nurse on staff.

In 2014, we partnered with Fair Trade USA to produce, as an experiment, nine yoga styles in a Fair Trade Certified factory in India. Here is how the program works: We pay a premium into an escrow account for every Patagonia item that carries the Fair Trade Certified label. A democratically elected committee of workers chooses how to spend the premium. Workers have spent the funds on cash bonuses but also on an on-site childcare center or things they could not otherwise afford, like bicycles for a quicker commute home. In Nicaragua, a Fair Trade committee voted to place bulk orders for rice and beans for all the factory's employees to cut the cost of their food staples in half.

As of this writing, 87 percent of our clothes are produced in Fair Trade factories and 64,000 workers benefit from the program. The premium we pay, totaling $4 million thus far, is distributed among all workers in a factory, not just among those who work on the Patagonia assembly lines. Our example has helped Fair Trade USA grow over the past decade. They have now reached the billion-dollar mark in contributions to workers. The workers like the program because it gives them personal agency in what traditionally has been a top-down environment. The employers like it because it raises workforce morale.

The next big task is to secure a living wage for all workers making Patagonia goods. Factories will have to raise prices to be able to pay a living wage or lose revenue and risk worker layoffs. Since factories pay the same wages for similar work done for multiple brands, all the brands must agree to pay more (a delicate step that opens companies to legal liability for price fixing).

As FLA and Fair Trade USA have been invaluable partners helping us improve social conditions in the supply chain, so Bluesign Technologies, an independent verification firm, has been vital to our efforts to minimize environmental harm from chemicals used in fabric production. It has been crucial for us to have their systematic help screening fabric chemicals as either blue, safe to use; gray, special handling required; or black, forbidden. The firm performs regular audits of its partners to improve environmental performance in five key areas: resource productivity, consumer safety, water emissions, air emissions, and occupational health and safety. We have to regularly report our progress to them and meet improvement goals to maintain our Bluesign partner status. In 2007, we were their first brand partner. Close to 1,000 brands, manufacturers, and chemical suppliers now partner with Bluesign, including nine of our top ten material suppliers.

Our Footprint documents what we've learned from partners like Bluesign, FLA, and Fair Trade USA, and shows Patagonia's ongoing discoveries of how to be a more responsible company. We talk about where we have failed. The site illuminates, rather than hides, the messy process of making things. The deeper we dig into our processes, the more we discover. What we learn we share, in the hope of being useful to others.

## Common Threads/Worn Wear

The fabric analysis we commissioned in the early 1990s, as a response to those employees who became sick in our Boston store, opened our eyes to the social and environmental cost of everything we made. Polyester proved to be a more benign fabric than chemically intensive cotton, but it still came from oil drilled from the ground. And if organic cotton was superior to its "conventional" counterpart, including Bt strains, it still used water that drew down aquifers or relied on irrigation supported by a concrete dam that choked off the life of fish.

We began to consider the "cradle to cradle" thinking of architect William McDonough, who believes that just as natural waste regenerates life, human-made products at the end of their time should be remade into new products, ideally of equal value. We need to reduce reliance on scarce resources and keep our used-up products out of American landfills or European and Japanese incinerators.

In 2005, we initiated the Common Threads Garment Recycling Program, inviting customers to send us their worn-out Capilene underwear, which we would send to our polyester supplier in Japan to melt down, then re-extrude as new fiber. We wanted to be able to take back, by 2010, any Patagonia product for recycling. Every season, our intake of used Patagonia products increased. By 2011, we could accept any worn-out Patagonia product for recycling or repurposing.

In the decade since, we have accepted any Patagonia clothes returned to us at the end of life. But what customers give back is only a small percentage of what we produce. We have also faced numerous challenges getting the returns out of our warehouse and transformed into new products.

In the best closed-loop system, as with our polyester underwear or fleece, the new fiber created from recycling the old maintains its value. But cotton and wool cannot be melted, only shredded, and the new fiber produced is not of equal value to the original. The coarse short fibers of recycled cotton can be made into jeans or a thick woodsman-style shirt-jacket but not a fine woven shirt. It took us years to learn how to recycle most forms of nylon. Although we've learned how to make wallets from used fishing waders and beer cozies from wetsuits, recycling backpacks and wheeled luggage remain a challenge to be solved.

We began to realize that, despite our progress, we were working backward. No one should have to recycle what should never have been made. As environmental activist Annie Leonard has said, in the *reduce, repair, reuse, recycle* mantra, there is a reason recycling comes last. If you want to reduce the environmental and social harm you do, the injunction to reduce comes first. Don't make what won't be useful

# DON'T BUY THIS JACKET

It's Black Friday, the day in the year retail turns from red to black and starts to make real money. But Black Friday, and the culture of consumption it reflects, puts the economy of natural systems that support all life firmly in the red. We're now using the resources of one-and-a-half planets on our one and only planet.

Because Patagonia wants to be in business for a good long time – and leave a world inhabitable for our kids – we want to do the opposite of every other business today. We ask you to buy less and to reflect before you spend a dime on this jacket or anything else.

Environmental bankruptcy, as with corporate bankruptcy, can happen very slowly, then all of a sudden. This is what we face unless we slow down, then reverse the damage. We're running short on fresh water, topsoil, fisheries, wetlands – all our planet's natural systems and resources that support business, and life, including our own.

The environmental cost of everything we make is astonishing. Consider the R2® Jacket shown, one of our best sellers. To make it required 135 liters of

## COMMON THREADS INITIATIVE

### REDUCE
**WE** make useful gear that lasts a long time
**YOU** don't buy what you don't need

### REPAIR
**WE** help you repair your Patagonia gear
**YOU** pledge to fix what's broken

### REUSE
**WE** help find a home for Patagonia gear you no longer need
**YOU** sell or pass it on*

### RECYCLE
**WE** will take back your Patagonia gear that is worn out
**YOU** pledge to keep your stuff out of the landfill and incinerator

### REIMAGINE
**TOGETHER** we reimagine a world where we take only what nature can replace

water, enough to meet the daily needs (three glasses a day) of 45 people. Its journey from its origin as 60% recycled polyester to our Reno warehouse generated nearly 20 pounds of carbon dioxide, 24 times the weight of the finished product. This jacket left behind, on its way to Reno, two-thirds its weight in waste.

And this is a 60% recycled polyester jacket, knit and sewn to a high standard; it is exceptionally durable, so you won't have to replace it as often. And when it comes to the end of its useful life we'll take it back to recycle into a product of equal value. But, as is true of all the things we can make and you can buy, this jacket comes with an environmental cost higher than its price.

There is much to be done and plenty for us all to do. Don't buy what you don't need. Think twice before you buy anything. Go to patagonia.com/CommonThreads or scan the QR code below. Take the Common Threads Initiative pledge, and join us in the fifth "R," to reimagine a world where we take only what nature can replace.

## patagonia®
patagonia.com

TAKE THE PLEDGE

*If you sell your used Patagonia product on eBay® and take the Common Threads Initiative pledge, we will co-list your product on patagonia.com for no additional charge.

© 2011 Patagonia, Inc.

This ad, produced by Patagonia, appeared
only once—in *The New York Times*, on Black
Friday 2011. PATAGONIA ARCHIVES

MEANINGFUL WORK

or won't last. Don't buy what you don't need. But how do you continue to increase your sales if you ask your customers to reduce their consumption while you, like any other product-producing company, need 3 percent annual growth just to stay even?

Once we got past the flinching that comes naturally when you pursue an idea that threatens to put you out of business, we refashioned our recycling program as the Common Threads Initiative, a partnership with our customers to pursue the four classic Rs in their proper order.

In 2011, inspired by a much earlier attempt from Esprit, we produced an ad for the Black Friday edition of *The New York Times* with the headline "Don't Buy This Jacket," asking customers not to buy what they don't need or what won't last. We promised, in turn, to redouble our efforts to make useful, long-lasting products.

We asked customers to first repair, before discarding or replacing, what breaks. In turn, we upsized our repair department to get the work turned around more quickly. We asked customers to recirculate what they no longer wore. We set up a platform to make it easier for customers to resell products, and we introduced used products for sale on our website. Would we lose business as a result? We wagered that if our customers were to buy more thoughtfully, and if we were to do our job well and make useful, high-quality products, they would continue to buy from us, and we'd gain new customers who shared our commitment.

Since then, we have expanded our business even as we've deepened the commitment to "take only what nature can replace," as we phrased it in the ad. The motto of our Worn Wear program, the successor to Common Threads, is "better than new." I remember my joy at driving *Delia*, our forty-year-old Worn Wear repair truck, up I-95 on an icy, windy March day from one event to another. At the University of New Hampshire and then the University of Vermont, I saw students lined up around the block to receive their single item of free gear—including expensive jackets and packs—with one stipulation. Each item needed a repair that the students had to do themselves, with a friendly instructive assist from a member of the Worn Wear crew. Toward the end of the day, I learned from a crewmember how to replace a broken buckle on my own pack, using a sharp seam ripper to detach the old and bright-red thread to sew on the new. A pack that had begun its life mass-produced in a factory has now become an individual talisman of my travels. I still use the pack every day.

Patagonia is moving steadily toward using only recycled and renewable raw materials. A decade ago, we couldn't use more than 60 percent recycled content in our polyester without sacrificing performance and durability. We could recycle only one kind of nylon. But, with our supply partners, we developed 100 percent recycled polyester that performs as well as that made from virgin oil.

We developed a nylon substitute for rain jackets and hat brims harvested from discarded fishing nets off the coast of South America. "Ghost" fishing nets are a major contributor to ocean pollution. Working directly with local fishers, our partner Bureo sorts, cleans, and shreds the nets at its facility in Chile; then recycles them into NetPlus, a 100 percent traceable postconsumer material. By turning fishing nets into fabric, we have helped keep more than 884 metric tons of plastic waste out of the world's oceans. Bureo's program also provides supplemental income for coastal communities.

We expanded the use of recycled content to natural fibers as well. Scraps collected from our sewing factories are mechanically shredded and spun into new yarn. We blend most of our recycled cotton with recycled polyester to produce sturdy sweatshirts and tees. Recycled cotton generates 80 percent fewer carbon dioxide emissions than conventional virgin cotton. We financed the development of machines to clean and recycle down. We now use recycled down (reclaimed from cushions and bedding) in more than forty styles, which reduces $CO_2$ emissions by 31 percent per kilogram of insulation.

Recycling poses big challenges, some of which are technical—a shirt contains different materials: cotton for the most part, but synthetic interfacing and plastic buttons have to be recycled separately. The recycler must also have a market for the recycled materials—or pay for their disposal.

But if we are to journey beyond the hamster wheel of consumerism, people will need to select new things to buy whose appeal—and usefulness—can survive the fading of their novelty. It's hard to believe that we can create an abundant economy with fewer, but better things, just as it's hard to imagine you can produce as much food on ten healthy acres as on 100 industrially planted acres that are barely alive.

## Growth

For most of its life, Patagonia has been a growing company, yet we have been able to make our practices more productive and less socially and environmentally extractive. Most businesses grow or decline (and some, like Levi Strauss, can be healthy decades after sales have peaked). Companies get sold. And they change if only to adapt to outside forces: social, cultural, and ecological.

But not all businesses rely on growth for business health. The Henokiens is an association of family-owned companies that have been in existence for more than 200 years. The oldest is Hoshi, a Japanese ryokan owned and managed since 717 by forty-six generations of the same family. Hoshi's success as an inn depends not on innovation, certainly not on growth, but on loving care of the local hot springs that have attracted customers for fourteen centuries. Other Henokiens include Beretta, the Italian arms manufacturer (1526); De Kuyper, a Dutch distiller (1695); a French music publisher (1772); an Italian cooper (1775); and the newest addition, an Austrian jeweler (1814). No longer a family-owned business, Patagonia will not be eligible to join the Henokiens.

We're not sure we could stay healthy as a business without growing at least as fast as inflation. But as a company seeking to be responsible, we treat a high rate of growth as a risky option not a necessity. Our business will always need to be seeded in some areas and pruned in others. Overall growth is not always a positive good, either for a company or for the world its actions impact.

## Collaborations

When Patagonia started to give 1 percent of sales to grassroots environmental organizations, we considered it our Earth tax. We knew that all the activities that went into making clothes bearing our label caused environmental harm. But we had no idea how to calculate that tax because we had no idea what our activities cost the planet. As we've said, most of that cost was in the supply chain, incurred by suppliers whose mills, dyehouses, and assembly factories we didn't own and whose actions we couldn't control.

Early on, we found other businesspeople who shared our environmental concerns: the owners of Ben & Jerry's and The Body Shop; and Paul Hawken, founder of an early natural-foods company called Erewhon, and then the gardening-tool company Smith & Hawken. Paul's 1993 book *The Ecology of Commerce* inspired the courtly Georgia carpet-tile manufacturer Ray Anderson, founder of Interface, to become, as *The Economist* noted in his obituary, "America's greenest businessman."

When we began to cast a cold eye on our own wasteful and polluting industrial practices, or those done in our name, we sought out and found other concerned apparel and footwear companies willing to offer advice and help. Often, they were much larger than us—like Levi Strauss, Nike, and Timberland.

From 2008 to 2012, we worked closely with Walmart, at their invitation, to share what we had learned in our smaller-company way about improving environmental practices. Walmart impressed us by the degree to which they could reduce their impact—and save millions of dollars in costs—through simple actions like removing excess packaging from deodorant sticks, concentrating laundry detergent in small bottles, and installing auxiliary power units in their trucks to reduce idling time.

Patagonia's talks with Walmart led to an unlikely David and Goliath collaboration. In 2011, Yvon and John Fleming, Walmart's chief merchandising officer, cosigned an invitation written on joint letterhead to attend the "21st Century Apparel Leadership Consortium" to be held in New York three months hence. They sent it to sixteen of the world's largest apparel companies, fifteen of whom accepted the call to establish a "universally accepted approach for measuring apparel sector sustainability, and to establish a strategy for ongoing collaboration to create and implement that standard."

The meeting resulted in the creation of the Sustainable Apparel Coalition (SAC), whose current membership generates more than a third of the apparel and footwear sold worldwide. The coalition adopted three goals: to annually measure the resource use of thousands of factories (to achieve reductions in water and electricity consumed and in waste and greenhouse gas emissions generated); rate the factories' labor practices and the environmental impact of the materials and processes they use; and create a consumer-facing index so that someone looking to buy a shirt could read from a hangtag's QR code a numerical rating of that shirt's social and environmental impact.

The Higg Index, now owned and managed independently of the SAC, also assesses the social and environmental impact of manufacturing, with a remarkable suite of tools for any consumer products company with a deep supply chain. The information that feeds Higg is currently self-reported; the next natural step, to establish a high level of citizen and government trust, would be to introduce independent verification to the process.

The consumer-facing element of the Higg Index was the slowest and most difficult to develop. Its introduction in 2021 met a negative response from some NGOs—and from the Norwegian government, which objected to its potential use as a greenwashing tool. Patagonia had its own reservations about the rating system, and we declined to participate in its first iteration.

One of the original intentions of the Higg Index was, in fact, to reduce the potential for greenwashing. The idea was that if competitors—Patagonia and Brand X—used the same metrics to rate the impact of our products, we would eliminate the temptation to beat our own drums to competing scientific claims.

The SAC does not rank the relative performance of its members. Nor does the Higg compare the performance of its clients. B Lab, however, works differently. Its B Impact Assessment (BIA) scores a business's environmental and social performance on a scale of 1 to 200. These scores, based on a company's governance and treatment of its stakeholders (employees, customers, communities, environment), are *public*. The average score of companies that take the initial self-assessment (150,000 companies as of 2023) is fifty-five. A threshold of eighty must be met before a company can be certified as a B Corp. Over the past decade, the assessment has become more rigorous rather than less, so it offers no easy path for companies interested solely in the badge.

We were initially reluctant to apply when we were approached by the B Lab founders, three college friends who had a personal motivation to "make business a force for good." Two of them had started, then sold, a basketball-shoe company. The partners had gone through, as we had at Patagonia, painful discoveries of their own social and environmental impact and worked to bring their values to bear on their practices. After selling the company, they were disappointed by the new owners' readoption of conventional practices and resolved to help other like-minded entrepreneurs stay the course. The basketball-shoe company went out of business, but B Lab is thriving.

We listened to the pitch but politely declined. We did not yet have the Higg to help us assess the impact of our products over their lifetime. We were just beginning work on the Footprint Chronicles, which outlined what we did and didn't know about our own practices, what we were proud of, and what we wanted to change. By then, we were already submitting to multiple audits of labor and environmental practices throughout our supply chain. We had already helped start the Fair Labor Association to audit labor conditions. We had been an early adopter of the independent Bluesign standard for chemicals used in our fabrics. (We have since helped create standards for responsible production of wool and down clothing and for regenerative organic agriculture.) We didn't see why we needed B Lab on top of the rest.

We decided to join up after the founders began to secure from state legislatures "benefit corporation" status for certified B Corps. A benefit corporation enshrines its core values and commitments in its business charter and articles of incorporation, creating a legal obligation that must be honored, particularly at any time of sale, when a company's founding values are at risk. In 2011, we certified as a B Corp, and on January 1, 2012, when California became the seventh state to confer a benefit corporation status, Malinda and Yvon were the first in line to sign the papers. Yvon wore a tie for the occasion.

Early on, we discovered some significant benefits to becoming a B Corp that we had not anticipated. The BIA tool provided the only holistic assessment of our work and impact, from the difference in pay between our highest- and lowest-paid employees to the use of permeable concrete in our parking lots.

Another benefit addressed the third and last clause of our purpose statement at the time: "Build the best product, cause no unnecessary harm, and *use business to inspire and implement solutions to the environmental crisis.*" B Corps comprise a community. We were now in the good company of businesses committed to acknowledging—and acting on—their social and environmental responsibilities. The actions of one inspire and embolden those of another. An owner or manager can call on a B Corp colleague to seek advice on solving a shared problem. And in addition to cooperation, some friendly competition is involved. Patagonia consistently scores in the top 5 percent of B Corps. Our last two scores, as of this writing, were over 150, 70 points above the baseline for joining. But Dr. Bronner's, the soap company, scored a whopping 206.7, causing us to scramble to find out what they knew that we hadn't yet discovered.

B Corps now number more than 6,400 companies in 159 industries and 89 countries. B Corps include Maker's Mark, Danone North America, Natura, and Nespresso. B Lab obliges its participants to become benefit corporations wherever they are legal, which means, for now, in forty-five states that have some variety of benefit corporation law on the books, and in France, Italy, Colombia, and Ecuador. The movement is growing rapidly, especially in Europe, Latin America, and the Caribbean.

## From Supporting Activists to Becoming an Activist Company

We had been a company that supported activists long before we became an activist company. We gave our annual 1 percent of sales to grassroots environmental organizations and earmarked generous space in our catalogs and on our website for environmental education, often on issues that didn't see much daylight elsewhere: the need for corridors for wildlife to roam, the truth about open-net-pen farmed salmon, the plight of the oceans, and the adverse environmental impacts of hydropower. We also engaged in a bit of activism of our own. Every two years we conducted a "Vote the Environment" campaign, encouraging fellow citizens to acknowledge the environmental crisis and address it at the ballot box. In the 2010s we started to publish

NEXT SPREAD The Valley of the Gods, sacred to the
Diné, was restored to the Bears Ears National Monument
by President Biden on October 8, 2021. San Juan
County, Utah. MICHAEL ESTRADA

MEANINGFUL WORK

books that celebrate the natural world (and the human experience of
nature) or promote an important environmental campaign.

The 2016 election of Donald Trump was an ice-water moment for
us, after so many positive events the previous year (the COP21 climate
agreement in Paris, the adoption of the UN Sustainable Development
Goals, and publication of Pope Francis's *Laudato Si'*).

We spent nearly $2 million in support of the effort to secure fed-
eral protection for the 1.9 million–acre Bears Ears region of San Juan
County, Utah, a space of extraordinary natural beauty and cultural
significance, with more than 100,000 ancestral sites sacred to five
tribes. Oil and gas and mining companies had become interested in
an area once considered too remote for development. In one of his
last acts as president, Barack Obama set aside 1.35 million acres as the
Bears Ears National Monument.

Eleven months later, Trump slashed the size of the monument by
85 percent, dividing it into two noncontiguous sections. A proposal to
reopen the Easy Peasy uranium and vanadium mine followed shortly.
Three separate groups filed lawsuits charging the administration
with violation of the American Antiquities Act. Patagonia was a party
to one of the suits, which were eventually rolled into one lawsuit.

We sued the government the same week the Thomas Fire upended
our main campus operations. The fire sped from ridgetop to ridgetop
over a stretch of fifty miles, threatening, over a two-week stretch, the
three communities (Ventura, Santa Barbara, and Ojai) where most
of our local employees live. Our main campus suffered more than $2
million in smoke damage. More than 75 percent of our local employees were displaced temporarily by fire or smoke, and some, three
months later, by the late-night mudslide that took twenty-three lives
in Montecito.

While the fire raged—in Ventura one day, then Santa Barbara, then
Ojai, and back to Ventura—staff in inventory management, finance,
logistics, and production would gather with their laptops in one

77

colleague's kitchen to get work done, and when the flames and smoke got closer, they'd move to the safety of another colleague's kitchen in another town. Some of these temporary measures became a three-year norm during the COVID shutdown.

The Bears Ears lawsuit was working its way through the federal court when Joe Biden was elected. On his first day in office, he ordered a review of Trump's decision, and ten months later restored Bears Ears monument to its original size. Today, the Bears Ears Inter-Tribal Coalition is working toward protection of the 600,000 acres in the ecosystem that are not yet part of the monument.

As we transitioned from being a company that supported activists toward becoming an activist company, we learned more about environmental injustice and racial marginalization, about the hollowing out of rural life to increase the wealth of very few people. We learned that we can no longer pursue activist solutions that advance the health of society at the expense of the wilderness, and vice versa.

This realization requires a radical rethinking of advocacy. Politicians, both Democrats and Republicans, have traditionally favored the interests of business against the health of the planet. Republicans have defended the right of capitalists to make money as they see fit, while Democrats have defended the rights of workers to good-paying jobs in extractive and polluting industries—planet be damned by both.

Environmentalists and conservationists have defended not so much the planet but the beauty and integrity of the wilderness. The conservation-minded didn't worry about how people made their living, or that the poor and marginalized, rural and urban, suffer first and most from the degradation of natural systems, both outside and inside areas that can still be named wild.

Our actions needed to reverse the decline of the natural world while advancing human well-being. We had limited time and money. So, how do we proceed?

General Dwight Eisenhower was responsible for strategy and logistics in the European theater during World War II, including the Normandy invasion on D-Day, which turned the tide in the Allies' favor. When asked the key to his success, Eisenhower said, "Whenever I run into a problem I can't solve, I always make it bigger. I can never solve it by trying to make it smaller." Business and government strategies must do the same. We will fail if we try to make the environmental crisis smaller by pursuing compromise between profit and purpose, between human and planetary health.

When, in 2018, Yvon simplified Patagonia's original statement of purpose, it was in the spirit of making the problem bigger, yet simpler. Patagonia workers were deeply connected to the old version: "Build the best product, cause no unnecessary harm, and use business to inspire and implement solutions to the environmental crisis." But Yvon distilled this principle to its crux: "We're in business to save the home planet." Environmental activism had become a job of salvage, not simply deterrence.

## Kernza

Topsoil is "black gold" that feeds the world and draws carbon out of the air and into the ground where it belongs. The fertile topsoil of the Great Plains once reached six feet deep. Starting in the 1870s, exports of its grain financed the industrialization of the United States and the launching of the modern world. That topsoil, like most throughout the world, is now a few inches thick, degraded by a century and a half of monocultural, industrial farming.

Patagonia had been friends for years with Wes Jackson, an agronomist whose life project has been the restoration of the Great Plains. Wes told us about a wheatgrass he had hybridized in the early 2000s called Kernza, whose roots extend nearly six feet down, branching out into the perfect environment for microbes

Luke Peterson measures the root depth of his Kernza plants, Madison, Minnesota. AMY KUMLER

and fungi to create topsoil much faster than nature can on her own. A perennial, Kernza does not have to be planted every year, minimizing tillage. When soil comes back to health, it requires much less water and fewer inputs, natural or otherwise. And healthy soil can absorb carbon from the atmosphere, and retain it, to help replace the carbon capture we have lost from cutting down the rainforests.

"Kernza sounds fantastic," we said. "Where can we buy some?"

"Oh, you can't buy Kernza," Wes said.

"Why not?"

"I can't get anyone to grow it."

"Why not?"

"There's no market for it. A farmer can't grow what he can't sell."

That made sense to us. So, we partnered with a brewery in Portland, Oregon, to create Long Root Ale with Kernza as the marquee ingredient, which enabled us to contract with a farmer in Minnesota to plant the first 100 acres. The ale sold out. More Kernza has been planted; we now include it as an ingredient in a pasta from Patagonia Provisions. Since then, cereal companies much larger than Patagonia have ordered more Kernza to be planted, to do carbon farming on their own.

Patagonia Provisions, launched in 2011, was tiny, what our former CEO Rose Marcario might have called "mouse nuts" on the balance sheet. But this small success with Kernza served as a compass for Provisions: Every new product would help solve a problem in the food system. It would be rich in nutrients, delicious, and improve its source of life, whether the soil, river, or ocean.

We partnered with Rodale and Dr. Bronner's to create a new certification for regenerative organic agriculture that concentrates on soil health. It also recognizes that soil can't be well cared for without healthy farmworkers and communities, and twenty-first-century animal welfare standards.

The Long Root Ale origin story reminds us that business, for all its flaws, can do tremendous good in a way other social sectors can't.

A government must support its activities through taxes, an NGO through tapping donors. But business can be generative and self-supporting at any scale of activity.

## Tin Shed Ventures

In 2013, we created Tin Shed Ventures, a small fund to invest in companies—mostly startups—that use business to reduce environmental harm and address the climate crisis. The fund (along with Patagonia Provisions) was an eye-opening departure from the familiar apparel business. Through Tin Shed, we discovered promising innovations, like turning supermarket waste into fuel and fishing nets into hat brims, as well as cleaning and recycling down from jackets and sweaters.

Tin Shed focuses on three areas of interest: regenerative organic agriculture and food supply, biodiversity monitoring and restoration, and supply-chain improvements. We invest long-term in companies whose values and managers we respect, and that don't demand fat, five-year returns or formulate an "exit strategy" in advance. Either scenario can derail a promising company from its responsible path and force a premature sale.

## Environmental Justice and Antiracism

The more we worked with minority groups fighting for the health of their land and communities, the more we understood that saving our home planet required the help of people of all races, classes, and zip codes. Our Grants Council added "front-line environmental justice" as its own category to support marginalized communities impacted by environmental degradation and pollution.

But we had much to do internally. Until recently, few people of color worked at our Ventura campuses except in the sample room

Antonio Bustos spreads out a nylon net near
San Vicente, Chile. JÜRGEN WESTERMEYER

or in childcare. Our athletic ambassadors in the United States and Europe—the faces on our website and in our films and journals—were largely white, as were the environmental grantees invited to our bi-annual Tools Conference.

During the summer of 2020, in the wake of the murder of George Floyd and amid the COVID pandemic, employees at Patagonia called on managers to make the company more representative of people of color: in hiring, in who is featured on the website. They called on our company to become more conscious of implicit bias on a campus much whiter than the population base.

We had advocated a living wage for workers in our supply chain, but now we made sure that we were paying a living wage to all our employees, including those who worked in retail, the café, and child-care. We began to hire, when hiring resumed, more people of color and in more responsible positions. We took guidance from a host of new community groups within the company to ensure that those new to our work culture felt welcome and included, with an equal sense of opportunity for recognition and advancement. For our website we sought out stories—there is no lack of them—from people who love the sports we love who are not white, straight, cisgender, or young.

For three decades we had shared four published core values: quality, integrity, environmentalism, and "not bound by convention." This last has always been the most popular among our employees. To these four, the employees now added a new value: justice, equity, and antiracism.

## Citizens, Consumers, Producers

As members of society, we are all citizens, consumers, and pro-ducers. As citizens, we can cast out tyrants. As consumers, we can refuse to buy crap that companies will have to withdraw from the market. However, it is in our productive role, nudged by enlightened consumers, that we make the biggest difference. Ninety percent of a product's environmental impact is committed at the design stage; two-thirds of waste is generated by industry, not by households—so what we do at work has far greater consequence than going out on a Saturday morning to trade in the Suburban for a Bolt.

+++

Meaningful work, what is it exactly? Regardless of our talent or education, our preference for working with words or numbers or with our hands, our ability to cut a pattern or lay out an ad or negotiate with a supplier, we have meaningful work at Patagonia because our company does its best to be responsible to nature and to people.

On the one hand mundane and often tedious, our daily gestures are on the other hand infused with the effort to give something useful and enjoyable to society without bringing undue harm to nature, the commons, or other workers. Everyone at Patagonia knows to take one step toward responsibility, learn something, then take another step. Many of our suppliers and customers have also become invested in this process of improvement. What engages us most deeply enlivens us. Lively, gratified workers make good business possible—they make it thrive.

# 3

# The Elements of Business Responsibility

Yvon has often said, sometimes ruefully, "Every time I do the right thing, I make money." He means that every time we refuse to do the wrong thing, the constraints we place on ourselves force innovations that result in products we otherwise wouldn't have developed. This has been true of organic cotton clothes, Yulex wetsuits, and jackets and hats with brims made of abandoned fishing nets. Our innovations gained us new customers and a good reputation—and built our business.

Patagonia has been an experiment, but every business has become one in this time of whipsaw change. How human beings make a living is in flux. What's certain is that any twenty-first-century business seeking to keep customers and make new friends will need to improve the environmental and social performance of its products. More customers will demand to know: Does your product or service hurt them or their children? Does your product hurt the workers who make it, or their community, or the ecology of the place where the product's components are drilled, mined, farmed, or stored? Is your product worth its social and environmental cost? It may arguably have a social benefit. But, unless we happen to sell organic seeds or night-soil compost, what we all do at work takes more from the Earth than it gives back.

In this time of existential threat, let's make things that fulfill human needs and make them so they last. Let's produce food in sensible quantities with strategic distribution to avoid so much waste. Half the food made in this country is not eaten and most clothing is thrown

Hub Hubbard, Patagonia's wetsuit designer, at the
drawing table, Ventura, California. TIM DAVIS

away while it has plenty of life left. No industrial economic system has yet moved any distance from the model of dig it up, use it, throw it away. Instead, we can "mine our waste," in the words of investor/conservationist Rick Koe, and turn it into things we need. We can shift from an extractive economy toward one that regenerates natural systems and human communities.

Many companies have begun to change, some to protect their reputation and others to reduce costs (energy, water, waste, and pollution are expensive). Some companies change because their employees demand it. Or they need to meet European standards, which are higher than American ones, to compete in a global market. Still others see opportunities to develop new markets: Young people want healthy, organic food; purchasing agents for public institutions have to meet new environmental mandates for trash receptacles and cafeteria napkins.

Every company has business partners with a stake in its success. The social and ecological footprint of one stakeholder reflects on the others; so, all have the potential—and the responsibility—to influence each other. REI can't tell Patagonia how to make jackets, but it doesn't have to buy from us either. If it cares about reducing the environmental impact of the jackets sold on its floor, REI can ask us to improve our practices, or buy from someone else who will. And they should.

Every company, more now than a decade ago, has to win the minds and hearts of its employees who consider it their birthright not simply to bring home a paycheck but to feel satisfied by the work they do. If companies earn their loyalty and engage their intelligence, today's workers will figure out, before the old economy caves in, how to lay the foundation and put up the roof and walls for the new. It takes more than competitive pay or humane employment policies to inspire employee commitment and trust. Not everyone can satisfy their heart's desire working for your company, but everyone could at least feel useful, and some even enlivened by what they do all day long. Employees who grew up in this century do not want to leave their values at home with the dog. They bring their whole selves to work. Many, even those who carry college-loan debt, will forgo working for a high-paying "bad" company in favor of a lower-paying business they respect.

What makes a company responsible? Should it have a healthy balance sheet, provide for the well-being of its employees, make excellent products, be a good force in the community, protect nature—and even revive or recharge natural systems? We think that a responsible company bears all these obligations. But before we get into the details of how business might deal with them, it would help to better understand how a company's responsibilities differ today from 50 or 150 years ago.

The responsible company of 1860 was one that paid a return to its shareholders, honored its commitments, and kept honest books. Only 5 percent of all work was done by machine; 95 percent was done by humans and animals. A hundred years later the picture had become far more complex. By 1960, the figures were reversed, and 95 percent of all work was performed by machines. It would take, if it were possible, the muscle power of 700,000 people to enable a jet to fly. Machines made us capable of accomplishing far more than we and our animals could ever have done on our own.

In the century between 1860 and 1960, limited liability for corporations became law to protect shareholders and officers from imprisonment or personal bankruptcy when their companies committed damage or fraud or failed to pay their bills. But companies took on new obligations to workers as well, thanks to the growing legitimacy and power of unions and progressive political movements in industrial countries. Corporations became liable for the health and safety of the workplace. Laws enacted, if not always enforced, limited working hours, particularly for women and children, in the United States and Europe, and later throughout most of the world.

The responsible company of 1960 (in the United States, examples included IBM, 3M, Bell & Howell, Cummins Engine, and Johnson

& Johnson) was big, rich, and going global. It kept honest accounts, hated to bribe officials, and paid its people decently (more decently its men, the better, it said, to support nonworking wives and children). It maintained substantial programs for job training, general education, and safety in the workplace; promoted from within; and supported community hospitals, schools, and nonprofessional sports activities.

The big responsible company in those days had a fixed and clear hierarchy—men were at the top and, in the United States and Europe, white. Its management philosophy drew from the West's earliest models for organizing large numbers of people through command and control: the military and the Roman Catholic Church, with new contributions from manufacturer Henry Ford and efficiency consultant Frederick Winslow Taylor. As they do now, the company's top executives took time out from their careers to serve in government. The company's board members also might have served on the boards of its major suppliers, customers, and banks without being challenged for conflict of interest. The company had sometimes adversarial, sometimes cooperative, relationships with its unions.

The standard of living for less-educated, lower-salaried or wage-earning employees relative to their bosses was higher than it is now. A substantial number of employees could confidently look forward to a company pension as well as a check from Social Security or, in other countries, its equivalent. A big company in those days was likely to be industrial, not financial; US commercial banks, after New Deal reforms, could not operate across state lines, own nonbanking operations, or combine with investment banks. Businesses were big and powerful, but smaller—and less rich and powerful—than today. The Dow Jones average on the last day of 1960 was 615.

Over the past sixty years, big business faced new regulations to prevent discrimination based on race, gender, and age. In the United States, Europe, and Japan, new environmental laws restricted air and water pollution. But as technology rapidly advanced, it put an end to several kinds of jobs and made many workers redundant. In the United States, according to one researcher, five out of six lost manufacturing jobs could be attributed to increased productivity. The remaining one out of six was lost mainly to offshoring, as China became the industrial heartland of the United States and much of the developed world.

While the Dow grew from 1,000 in 1982 to 14,000 in 2007, this fabulous increase in wealth rewarded the top 10 percent of earners far more than the middle class—especially in America and Britain. Although middle-class real earnings did not grow, net worth did for those with 401(k) accounts and real estate holdings. As income plateaued, the two-worker family became the norm, the two-parent family less so. Social safety nets began to fray throughout the most industrially advanced countries, such as Europe and Japan, as fewer workers paid taxes to support a growing number of retirees. In companies espousing shareholder primacy, a reptilian indifference took hold: customers, employees, suppliers, community, nature be damned. Stock price wasn't everything, it was the only thing.

By most visible measures—cleanliness of the air and water—the health of the environment in developed countries improved in those years, graced by the passage of major environmental laws in the 1970s. Angelenos could now see the San Gabriel Mountains on a summer day. The Cuyahoga River no longer caught fire. Anadromous fish returned to the Hudson and Kennebec Rivers (though you were warned not to eat them).

The less visible, less malodorous problems worsened in the form of elevated greenhouse gases and depletion of water and soil; until, in the 2010s and 2020s, they became glaringly obvious in the form of higher temperatures, fiercer storms, and rising seas. More than a billion people now live in areas threatened by desertification.

World population in 1860 was about 1.25 billion; by 1960, three billion. By 1973, when Patagonia started business, population had risen to nearly four billion. Fifty years later, it has passed eight billion.

Fred White, artist and now director of a reuse center, brings a vintage piece of clothing back to life during his previous tenure as a manager for Patagonia's New York City stores.  DREW SMITH

Nearly two-thirds of the US economy relies on consumer spending, a higher percentage compared to other developed countries. Editorial pundits from the bourgeois-bohemian center-left of *The New York Times* to the troglodytic hard right of *The Wall Street Journal* bow to the god of consumer spending and its gospel of growth. But growth of what? Poke your nose into any store in the mall and look around. Much of what we produce to sell to each other to earn our living is crap, high and low. There are the ever-more-luxurious, specialized goods, like electronic temple massagers and personal oxygen bars and cheap junk food and disposable clothing.

Manufactured goods come with a cost that exceeds their price tag. Much of the useful stuff, such as tool sets, appliances, and lounge chairs, is cheaply made and won't last. Much of what does last—switch plates and spatulas—is made of virgin plastic that persists in the environment long after it is no longer useful. Every piece of manufactured junk contains within it something of the priceless: applied human intelligence and spirit for one thing, natural capital for another—something from the forest or a river or the soil that cannot be replaced as fast as we extract it. We're wasting our brains and our one and only natural world on the design, production, and consumption of things we don't need, aren't good for us or the planet, and are not worth the money.

The days of our low-quality, high-consumption society are numbered, as resources grow scarcer, and the world population grows bigger and more urban. We are in transition toward the recovery of our collective senses—our sense of time, of public space, of proportion. A responsible company in the twenty-first century needs to cultivate an economy based on fewer things of better quality.

It makes sense to make a hammer or a sewing machine that will last a lifetime, redesign a bicycle to be both lighter and stronger, or recycle an old down jacket by repurposing its components with the thoroughness a Japanese chef would bring to employing every part of a fish. Living in a world of fewer, better things that reflect their true social and environmental cost may prompt us to shop less as a form of entertainment. That wouldn't be so bad. We might recover time to pursue other deep interests and pleasures, and have more time with our friends and family.

Of course, there are other, more dystopian possibilities: Jeff Bezos or Elon Musk would have us colonize Mars to escape the despoliation of Earth; Mark Zuckerberg would have us stay home and retreat into the metaverse, which we could navigate through a cartoon avatar that "self-expresses" our own facial features. In the metaverse, we could dress our avatar in expensive digital designer clothes that keep nobody warm, paid for with our nonvirtual credit card.

Those clothes may not be made of material, but they bear material costs. The artificial intelligence (AI) models used for the metaverse emit massive amounts of $CO_2$ emissions. During a global chip shortage, the metaverse is competing with the electric vehicle industry to get semiconductor components—and winning; it is swelling the energy consumption and emissions of data centers.

Dystopia is not inevitable. But it will take all the intelligence and navigational skill we can muster to collectively rebuild the house while living in it. It will require all the heart we have in us to care for each other as we shift from an economy that worked for many—and for some of us splendidly—to one where no twelve-year-old works a sewing machine and lives on a bowl of rice a day, and no Asian river flows into a sea dyed indigo from the local jeans factory.

Companies, large and small, can be essential to a postconsumerist society—a society where people consume, yet the well-being of the planet and populace has priority over shopping. We will continue to need food, clothing, and shelter, as well as fun and games, and we need to organize ourselves to provide them. We will need energy to stay warm in cold weather and cool in hot. But we are beginning to understand the true cost—social, ecological, economic—of everything we make. We need to make less, and whatever we make should be high quality and long-lasting to better offset its social and environmental cost. The goal is not simply to reduce, but to eliminate that cost by becoming a self-sustaining, regenerative economy and planet.

A word about a word we've chosen to use as little as possible: sustainability, which means not taking more from nature than we can give back. As yet we all still take more than we give. No human economic activity is sustainable. We believe we have no right to apply that word to our business activity until work does not interfere with nature's capacity to regenerate itself and support a rich variety of life. Responsible seems to us to be the more apt, modest word while we hasten toward a restorative rather than an extractive economy.

+++

We've now come to the heart of our book, where we'll lay out the elements of business responsibility, as we see them, to five key stakeholders: owners/shareholders, workers, customers, the community, and nature as a whole.

## Responsibility to Owners/Shareholders

Fifty years ago, the authors of this book had lunch together at Myrt's Cottage Café, a greasy spoon a block away from the shop, staffed by beehived waitresses who, for decades, had served biscuits and gravy to workers in the nearby oil field. Johnny Cash may have come here for coffee and a smoke in the 1950s, when he lived up the road and played the honky-tonk across the street.

At the time of our workingman's lunch, Yvon, the company owner, was paying himself $800 a month and I, his twenty-one-year-old nephew, was taking in $2.25 an hour to answer the phone, pack boxes, and type invoices. As a non-surfer, I was one of two people left in the office whenever the waves were firing. Recently promoted to sales manager, with an hourly raise to $3.00, I told Yvon, "That sounds good, but what does a sales manager do?" Yvon shrugged and said, "Figure it out."

Over lunch at Myrt's, we tried to figure out what it took to make a living selling apparel in the United States. We talked about doing what people were telling us we had to do to become more of a real business—hire reps, issue catalogs, exhibit at a trade show, maybe take out a couple of ads.

At one point, Yvon turned to me and said, "If I did everything right, did everything the experts say I have to do to succeed in business, I'd go broke."

Around that time, an old garmento told us a legend about how to make money in clothing: First, you remove the paper pattern, called the marker, that lies on top of a fabric stack to guide the cutter. Then, you crumple or "shrink" the marker, place it back on the fabric, and run the blade. That half a percent of fabric you save becomes your profit. Scary advice.

Those stories come back to us now, as we write this book and discuss what a responsible company does or doesn't do. A company that aims to be socially and environmentally responsible has the same primary duty as any other company: to pay its bills on time. It cannot honor its other responsibilities unless it meets its first responsibility: to be financially fit.

That said, shareholder return should not be piratical. Profit as the sole purpose of a business enterprise is no better for the business's health than it is for the health of the planet. Excess profit raked from the table by shareholders comes at the expense of investment in employees, systems, and R & D and leaves a company dependent on growth to make up the difference. How much business can be done in how short a time becomes the aim of the enterprise, rather than quality or customer relationships that serve long-term business health—and, coincidentally, human and planetary health as well. For the publicly traded company maximizing profits, stock price becomes the most important product.

But the balance sheet still counts. The word is apt. Unbalanced business leads to distracted managers who flail about with a runaway firehose rather than productively meeting the company's needs and developing its opportunities. Does what you bring in exceed what you owe? Are you getting paid so you can pay your bills? Do you have enough put aside for a rainy (or fiery) day? Is inventory flowing properly or bottlenecking? Are you spending too much on x and too little on y?

Are you investing in product innovation? This question is key for companies seeking to improve their social performance and reduce their environmental impact. You can't do what lazy companies do— bleed suppliers for cost reductions to achieve greater efficiency or use cheaper but more environmentally harmful, often labor-exploitative, materials to put more money in the bottom line. You and your people must figure out the right thing to do in the right way and then go about it, gradually if you must, but never losing sight of the endgame, which is to keep the quality of your products high while satisfying your stakeholders, one of whom is the Earth.

Today, though, you can't measure the true health of a business. Luca Pacioli, the brilliant Venetian monk who invented the balance sheet (he also tutored Leonardo da Vinci in math), did not factor into his new system what contemporary economists call "externalities," everything a company does that someone else has to pay for—socialism for capitalists. Externalities include community blight when an employer moves on, or a company's contribution to atmospheric carbon or to oceanic gyres of degraded plastic the size of Texas. Nor can any company measure with statistical rigor what it gives back to a community or nature.

PEOPLE

SOCIAL VARIABLES
community, education, equity,
social resources, health, well being,
and quality of life

BEARABLE

EQUITABLE

SUSTAINABLE

ENVIRONMENTAL
VARIABLES
natural resources,
water and air
quality, energy
conservation
and land use

VIABLE

ECONOMIC
VARIABLES
the bottom line
and cash flow

PLANET

PROFIT

Not that resourceful people haven't tried over the past thirty years to develop more comprehensive metrics. Hazel Henderson called for a redefinition of gross domestic product (GDP) capable of tracking—and summing up—social and environmental performance as well as sales. But governments still measure any addition to GDP as positive, whether the product is a land mine or a Bible. The sales of both are faithfully registered as an economic plus, regardless of their impact.

Building on Henderson's work, John Elkington in 1994 coined the phrase triple bottom line (TBL) to measure indicators of an individual company's social (human capital) and environmental (natural capital) performance, as well as profit (financial capital). Elkington intended

TBL as a metric that could then be rolled into a newly redefined GDP to chart the world's true economic health rather than the sum of its sales. Elkington's idea was influential. In 2007, the United Nations ratified TBL as a standard for public-sector accounting to measure the true cost of government subsidies to industry.

But in 2018, Elkington issued a "recall" of his idea, saying it needed re-evaluation. What he had intended as a "genetic code, a triple helix of change for tomorrow's capitalism, with a focus on breakthrough change, disruption, asymmetric growth (with unsustainable sectors actively sidelined), and the scaling of next-generation market solutions" had devolved into a marketing tool without precision. Companies could enumerate their financial impact, but not so easily the social and environmental value they added or destroyed. The non-financial components lacked both rigor and a universal standard. The difficulty should not be underestimated. We have had double-entry bookkeeping for 500 years. We have had less than half a century to learn—and agree on—how to measure what a company, or nation, adds to or subtracts from nature and the commons. As yet no accounting device (with the possible exception of the B Impact Assessment) holistically measures the health of a business, let alone a national or global economy.

Absent a B Corp score, a responsible company's rigorous accounting tools are limited to its financial health. But even these tools have their drawbacks, as Tensie Whelan at New York University's Stern School of Business has noted. Currently, only capital expenditures for long-term assets are amortized, so their cost doesn't hit the bottom line in a single fiscal year.

At Patagonia, many of our environmentally beneficial moves—beginning with the switches from pitons to chocks and conventional to organic cotton—lost money for a time, but then became a strong new source of profit. Doing the right thing made money, just not the next day. We initially viewed these moves as risks we were willing to

Hector Castro and his daughter mark out the repair work to be done at Patagonia's wetsuit repair facility, Ventura, California.  KYLE SPARKS

take; in hindsight, they were investments. We can amortize capital expenditures for buildings and childcare vans but not for staffing a new childcare center. That line item can be budgeted only as a profit-diminishing expense, even if we can make an educated guess, based on experience, that overall employee retention and engagement will increase, which in turn reduces costs for the succeeding years.

Environmental cost reductions for energy, water, and waste often fatten the bottom line but social investments don't. Much of what counts is yet to be measured. We'll speak more to this issue in the next chapter.

Meanwhile, companies will do whatever they have to do to meet payroll. Increasingly, however, they will also have to assign measurable value to their social and environmental impacts or face the cruel surprise of losses in staff morale and "ecosystem services": That's when the best employees quit, and the price of fossil fuels goes up as the availability of fresh water goes down.

## Responsibility to Your Workers

The responsible company owes its employees light-handed yet attentive management, financial transparency, encouragement to cooperate across departmental divisions and continuously improve processes, freedom to organize workflow with minimal delays or interference from higher-ups, and a penalty-free whistle to blow against wrongdoing.

The Industrial Revolution, which has now extended its reach to all the world, famously abstracts labor, whether the economy is organized along primarily capitalist or socialist lines. Few workers in either system own their own tools, bear full responsibility for their final product, or know the boss who benefits from their productivity. Meanwhile, companies rely less and less on people and more on AI and robots for large-scale manufacturing.

But even automated factories need people to run the robots. All companies seeking to boost productivity need the loyalty, dedication, and creativity of their human employees. The company's responsibility, then, extends to everyone in the supply chain who helps make or sell its product.

To fully engage workers and minimize both the balk and bulk associated with bureaucracy, larger companies must figure out how to best organize productive working groups of different sizes for different ends. Twelve is a good number for a small group to bond and work in concert to achieve a specific task with minimum hierarchy (think of a jury, a tribal hunting party, or an army squad). Anthropologist Robin Dunbar cites 150 as the magic number for community cohesion, based on the number of human relationships the human brain can handle. When it builds a new plant, the manufacturer W. L. Gore & Associates puts in 150 parking spaces. When the plant exceeds that capacity, the company builds a new one. Microsoft and Intel also limit the number of employees per building to 150, though they both run plants with multiple buildings. Hutterites, a communal religious group, form a new community when they reach that number. Along the same lines, a military company comprises between 80 and 225 people.

At Patagonia, we've noticed changes in cohesion when we move different departments to different floors and buildings. Adjacency matters: Situating our environmental team next door to the CEO engendered a certain dynamic; the CEO at the time became more environmentally educated and committed. When the enviros moved next to marketing, our storytelling improved. It was a boon to have the kids' playground adjacent to reception.

But a department can have only so many immediate neighbors at one time. People at Patagonia form important cross-departmental friendships, trade knowledge, and brainstorm product or other business ideas in our café, on lunchtime runs, and among fellow parents using Patagonia's childcare. Don't underestimate the conversations about work that happen casually; they can lead to significant advances for the company. It's important to create comfortable spaces throughout the campus for employees to gather in small groups of two and three, as well as more formal meeting rooms.

Informality has informed our business from the start. Chouinard Equipment for Alpinists, Patagonia's predecessor, was, as we mentioned, a throwback to the early Industrial Revolution. Our blacksmith shop housed equipment: a drop hammer, an anvil, a coal forge, jigs for drilling aluminum chocks, but no time clocks or assembly lines. Everyone was poor and most lived marginal, if well-traveled, lives. For a while, we paid a 10 percent bonus to anyone who took the initiative to work forty hours a week, a practice that turned out to be illegal; we were busted and required to stop. We partied heartily. The sheds faced a courtyard where we celebrated almost any event with an asado of barbecued lamb and a keg.

When we became a clothing company, and as sales increased, we had to become more professional, a process that at first consisted of throwing bright but inexperienced young people into new jobs to see if they could learn what we needed to know how to do.

We paid fairly well, considering the inexperience of our employees. We provided health insurance, although we did not have to; introduced childcare and parental leave; never made anyone "dress" for work (although new hires from the professional world had to learn how to dress down to fit in). People were free to take a long break midday to go surf or run, with the understanding that they'd come in early or stay late if needed to get the work done.

Our worst day as an employer came in 1991, when we laid off 150 employees. For two years we had managed the company too carelessly, bought too much inventory, sold too little of it, hired too many people, and salted away too little money to pay for an expansion that our bank cheerfully financed until they got into troubles of their own and pulled the plug. Costs had to go down and fast. After weeks of considering alternatives (like a shorter workweek, combined with a cut in pay), we decided to let go of 20 percent of our people—and all on the same morning to reduce the duration of the toxic atmosphere that persists when layoffs are expected. A consultant advised us how to handle the logistics: all day long employees watched their colleagues get called out for a talk and return without a job. By ten o'clock, employees had started to recoil and roll back their chairs at the sight of a manager re-entering the room to approach the desk of yet another fellow worker. I remember the looks on their faces because I was one of the managers laying people off and handing them their packets as they walked out the door.

We should note the bracing fact that, right after the layoffs, morale improved among the workers still with us. The hovering ax had fallen; those of us left still had our necks. We were a much more sober lot, absent the intoxication of growth, and more focused. We knew what we had to do to bring the business back to financial health, and we did it.

Our emergency plan for a downturn of any magnitude now is to cut the fat, freeze hiring, reduce travel, and trim every type of expense except salaries and wages. We've done this for short periods several times—once right after 9/11. If things get worse, we eliminate bonuses, which we have done once in thirty years. We paid them retroactively the following year when the picture brightened and we had profits to distribute.

If things get worse still, decisions get tougher. Half of our expenses are labor. Before we would cut anyone else's pay, we would reduce the salaries of managers, directors, vice presidents, and the top executives, including the owners. Then we would shorten the workweek and reduce pay accordingly. Only as a last resort, if we were in the deepest sort of trouble, would we again downsize the company with a general layoff.

These steps apply to common-variety downturns. When the COVID pandemic hit, and a few days before California's governor ordered everyone to stay home, we closed our warehouse—as well as our offices and stores—until we could rejigger space and systems so that pickers, packers, and shippers in Reno could work at least six feet apart from one another. The total US shutdown lasted seven weeks. Our Ventura offices were closed for two years. Over the summer of 2020 we, like other employers, were able to get government assistance for store and other employees we laid off or those we kept on at reduced hours and lower pay. Take-home pay for most workers stayed the same or was slightly reduced. Most highly paid employees took a temporary one-third pay cut. When the government assistance ended that fall, we offered voluntary retirement for some office and warehouse workers. It was not yet safe to reopen stores, so we did so gradually. In the meantime, we redeployed as many store staff as possible as remote-working customer-service reps for e-commerce. Direct sales boomed for us, as for others.

Post-pandemic, we require most Ventura staff to work on-site three days a week. We learned during COVID both how much we all need extra flexibility and how much we missed being together face-to-face in three dimensions.

Over the coming decade we will, like all companies, need to be nimble enough to navigate new "natural" disasters—weather chaos, pollution, shortages, viruses—while owning our responsibilities to our workers and fellow human beings. Patagonia is committed to paying a living wage to everyone who works or produces for us, including independent farmers and employee caregivers in our childcare centers. All employers should expect increasing pressure from workers and worker advocates to pay a living wage. Whether or not they want to, or think it's the right thing to do, they will soon have little choice.

It was assumed, as late as the 1960s, that the annual pay of one wage earner (usually male) should support his family. In the United States today, living-wage methodologies vary, but most assume that two workers will support a family of four. To meet even this more modest goal requires further increases in productivity, most of which will come from automation, which further depresses employment: More workers will be better paid, yet more people will be out of work.

The rise in unemployment could be avoided if there is a corresponding rise in labor-intensive, local jobs in agriculture and handicraft industries, or a shorter workweek. One recent study showed that a four-day workweek (which Patagonia has not adopted) boosts both productivity and morale. Policymakers could help through the negative income tax (NIT) or its structural equivalent, universal basic income (UBI). Milton Friedman popularized the NIT, and it was supported by Friedrich Hayek and presidential opponents Richard Nixon and George McGovern.

Dean Carter, who led our people and culture team (formerly HR) for several years, once noted that in the employer-employee relationship, viewed by law as "at will" (with either party free to leave), disproportionate power always rests with the employer. This is true at Patagonia. Our policies are generous and humane. We still let most employees go surfing during the workday. We send a company-paid caregiver with managers who are new mothers on business trips and provide paid maternity and paternity leave. But we can do better.

To help our home planet come back to life, and stay afloat as a business, Patagonia needs to engage the imagination and cultivate the entrepreneurial spirit of all our workers. Over the next decade, we will need to put even more emphasis on respect, reciprocity, and collaborative disruption. More decisions will need to be made, and made intelligently, at ground level. And, in service to our communities, and because it's the right thing to do, we need to draw our team from all races and economic classes. No company in our time can be successful for long without the respect of its workers, which it earns by respecting them in turn.

## Responsibility to Your Customers

The responsible company owes its customers safe, high-quality products and services; this applies to both basics and high-end goods. Goods need to perform well, but also be durable, easily repaired, and recyclable. Marketing claims, especially those for health and environmental benefits, should be made responsibly.

How do you gain a customer and keep one? First, make something or offer a service someone can use, and for which satisfaction endures. Second, romance, but do not bullshit, the people whose business you solicit.

Paul Hawken, when he was running Smith & Hawken during the 1980s, told us he didn't like to advertise because he didn't want "that kind" of relationship with his customers. He was referring to the alternate-reality environment of the ad, in print or on-screen, wherein a business bullhorns its message near other unrelated voices barking their own individual messages—like a bazaar but without the smell of spices and the snake dance.

Since the 1980s, commerce has greatly expanded. Marketing is noisier, more difficult to make fun of, and even harder to trust. More products have become disposable; more customers experience increasing frustration when a flimsy product fails, and they must deal with the customer-service rep on the scratchy line from the offshore call center, who has no authority to correct a problem and, instead, didactically repeats the company's rules until the line drops.

If the chase for cheaper labor is playing out to its conclusion, so is the corollary race to attract customers by price alone, when the product won't last, and the service won't deliver. Any customer can go online and find the cheapest price for anything anywhere in the world. And any customer dissatisfied with a product or service can post it to a blog. On that blog, they can question the way a chicken was raised, or a sweatshirt was sewn.

A one-of-a-kind jacket outside Patagonia's pop-up Worn Wear store in Boulder, Colorado.  KERN DUCOTE

To turn for a moment to romance: Selling and marketing seek to incite desire, but a company must love to sell something its customer loves to buy. For both ethical and practical reasons, the selling story, to paraphrase Mark Twain, must be mostly true. A company needs to present itself well to the customer; it may even preen a little, the way a lover might take care to dress for a date. A life story, or product story, told just this side of mythmaking is okay when it fairly represents what's real. But beware of conjuring a false image of your company's goods or services. Mystification will no longer work in a world where stage fog can be quickly dispersed by a competitor, activist, or regulator. Mystification is the opposite of transparency, which is a prerequisite for the common language we need if we are to save the planet.

Customers are expensive to find and to replace; they will only become more so. The responsible company treats the customer as a friend and equal who shares a love of what the company offers. The wooing of customers can be assigned a cost per thousand exposures, scaled, and tested. But the relationship, once sealed, is intimate. It cannot be abstracted or reduced to a transaction without risking the goodwill that is your company's most important asset.

The *duration* of the relationship is contingent on the company's ability to provide more things the customer needs and on the customer's ongoing confidence. The responsible company continues to state its case: It provides the best information it can on why its products or services meet a need, how those products are made, how long they'll last, what the customer must do to make them last longer with less environmental impact, and, finally, what to do with them when they reach the end of their useful life with that customer.

Emmanuel Faber, during his tenure as CEO of Groupe Danone, a Paris-based conglomerate of major food brands including Dannon yogurt and Evian water, committed the whole company to becoming a B Corp, beginning with its new US subsidiary, Danone North America. At the 2017 event celebrating B Lab's certification, Faber credited his commitment to pursue B Corp status to Patagonia's "Don't Buy This Jacket" ad. He said it taught him that you could appeal to customers on the basis of values rather than instincts.

## Responsibility to the Community

Your community comprises people living in proximity to your company and all those who supply it, wherever they live. The responsible company is a local asset wherever its people gather for work in offices, stores, warehouses, factories, and fields and orchards. A company's obligation to the community includes paying its fair share of taxes to support the services it relies on from the community (in schools, roads, utilities, health, and safety). A responsible company supports civil society with cash donations and in-kind contributions of product or services. Many companies, including Patagonia, now invite their satellite locations to have a say in local giving.

Suppliers are critical partners in improving the social and environmental performance of your products. With supply chains so deep, it is difficult to know, much less understand, their workings. But when you know who does what and where, you can work with your suppliers more intelligently and productively; you can also improve their working conditions and environmental stewardship. The quality of your suppliers' lives and work defines your products.

Traditionally, responsible companies have long supported their communities' hospitals, schools, and arts organizations. The best companies also recognize their significance to the economic health of their communities and avoid closing their doors—or help soften the impact of closing—by phasing out rather than shutting down operations, offering generous severance pay to laid-off workers, and supporting the community institutions that aid the unemployed.

Community also includes trade associations, NGOs, standards-setting organizations, nonprofits, and other citizens' organizations

Belinda Baggs and an activist friend paddle out at Torquay, Australia, to oppose oil drilling in the Great Australian Bight.
EMMA BÄCKLUND

that have an interest in what your company does. Advocacy groups may confront you about your practices, as may individual citizen activists through social media. Friendly or not, those who engage with you are part of your community in its broadest sense and require your attention. Trade associations and third-party verification organizations will become more important as more companies benchmark their social and environmental performance. Even in highly regulated industries, third party–validated internal or industrywide measurements are essential to the continuous improvement of business and regulatory practices.

For 200 years, industrial capitalism has disrupted and destabilized both the countryside and the urban neighborhood. Capitalism's siren song of relative prosperity lures the peasantry into town with the promise of wealth and ease, but often delivers instead, especially for that first generation off the farm, hard urban poverty and meaningless work. And a rise in the standard of living for one generation is no guarantee for the next. Downward mobility within families has become far more common than our myths reflect.

The rising tide may lift boats, but it also washes over neighborhoods, leaving hardship in its wake. In the United States, we now live with a level of inequality found elsewhere only in the developing world. We have nearly abandoned Midwestern counties and dilapidated American city centers, while in certain zip codes the restaurant with a hot new chef offers thousand-dollar wines and families of four live in houses big enough for twenty. The locally owned stores in poorer rural communities have shuttered their windows, displaced by a "dollar store" in town or the big-box mall off the interstate. In a poor urban neighborhood, checks are cashed for an exorbitant fee and the local grocer carries no fresh fruit or vegetables; the supermarket, which does, is an hour's bus ride away.

What businesses do matters to communities. A company's decision to put down roots or pull out directly hurts or helps the local citizens from Palo Alto to Greenwich, from Detroit to Smyrna. Every company needs to ask itself: Where are we local? And what are our obligations to those places we call home?

Patagonia's homes are wherever we have a concentration of employees—as we do in Ventura, Reno, Yokohama, and Amsterdam—and to a lesser but significant extent, wherever we have stores, more than seventy locations worldwide. We help make each store local by giving it an annual budget for grants to local environmental groups; as previously noted, recipients are determined by employee vote. Although we are not a significant employer for any community except Ventura and Reno, we are mindful in all our satellite locations of how what we do affects local housing, traffic, infrastructure, water, and habitat. Along with maintaining relationships with local environmental groups, we participate in beach and creek cleanups and habitat restoration. Online, Patagonia's Action Works platform links environmental grantees with local customers who want to volunteer their time or donate money.

We now know that good companies work with their stakeholders to build mutual trust within a community to solve local problems. To forgo the extractive, transactional profit that delivered uneven wealth across the globe for 200 years is to build new wealth based on mutual need and aspiration—on Emmanuel Faber's "values rather than instincts."

Businesses, like individuals, have the right to be responsible to their community. Acting on behalf of our threatened planet is both a condition and an expression of freedom—of what makes us human. As climate change's consequences become impossible to ignore, let alone deny, we also know that wealth itself cannot fully protect anyone from droughts, floods, and wildfires. Nor can wealth alone restore our oceans, rivers, and soil to health. Corporate shareholders will eventually, if in many instances begrudgingly, have to honor and act on what Haida leader Gerald Amos called "the right to be responsible."

## Responsibility to Nature

Nature decides our fate but has no voice of her own, at least not one that we hear. We can't sit with her at the table and ask her what she needs to get her work done or what she cares about most. In the face of nature's silence, business must honor the "precautionary principle," now embedded into law in the European Union and other countries; it states that, in the absence of scientific certainty, the burden of proof that a new product or technology is safe now falls on business.

The precautionary principle obliges us to reverse our centuries-old habit to act now and deal with the consequences later. Its corollary, the Science Based Targets initiative (SBTi), provides 3,000 participating companies with a methodology for reducing greenhouse gas emissions in line with COP21 goals.

An interesting development of the past decade: New Zealand and Canada have enshrined into law the rights of rivers to flow (though the rights to the water within their banks still belong to human "owners"). Ecuador and Bolivia incorporated the rights of nature into their federal constitutions. Launched in 1972 with Christopher Stone's essay "Should Trees Have Standing?" the "rights of nature" movement advocates legal rights for ecosystems around the globe, including Pittsburgh, where it was used to outlaw fracking and mining. Ecosystems, lawyers can now claim in many courts, have the right to thrive, regenerate themselves, and evolve naturally in tandem with human beings, who act as interdependent biotic citizens.

We know instinctively we are not superior to nature, but our language says otherwise. We refer to nature as "resources," as if it were at our disposal. We call nature our "environment," as if nature were here to wrap itself around us. We call ourselves "stewards," as if we have been ordained to be nature's keeper, a big key dangling from our neck, a white towel slung over the arm.

Our first responsibility is to be humbler, yet also more confident. We are a part of nature; we can learn to live on our planet without spoiling it. It is likely that we have an intrinsic role to play as part of the ordering and creativity of nature. Sweet, if that were true. And if it isn't true, our obligation doesn't change. Our survival depends on not spoiling nature.

Whenever and wherever we can, we need to leave nature alone. We all know when we see a patch of land that should be left wild or a stretch of water that should be freed from the chokehold of a dam that has outlived its purpose. Nature can deploy its own immense restorative powers once the assault is halted.

As we have argued throughout this book, beyond advocating and voting for legislation that looks out for our planet, our immediate responsibility is to reduce the harm we do in our daily work and take cradle-to-cradle responsibility for what we make and what bears our name.

The task for all of us during the next half century will be to scale the industrial model down rather than up. There are strong reasons to decentralize the energy grid so that when a crow fries a transformer in Alberta, it doesn't silence a sound stage in Los Angeles. And there is no reason to believe that a corporate monoculture is any healthier for economic life than an agricultural monoculture is for ecosystems.

Rising costs will constitute their own pressure on companies to adopt more diversified, locally driven practices. Expenses will rise for natural resources (especially energy and water) and for waste disposal. Companies, not individuals, generate 75 percent of the trash that reaches the landfill or incinerator. Packaging, for which companies are responsible, is disposed of almost instantly by the consumer and makes up a third of all waste.

Increased cost, if nothing else, obliges companies to understand and manage the environmental impact of products from their origins as raw materials through their manufacture, useful life, and eventual disposal. A product life cycle needs to be circular. Far better to use your own or another company's waste as feedstock than to use virgin materials.

A product at the end of its life can be broken down to create a new product of equal value. Where that's not possible, it can become a "raw" material for someone else's product. This requires collaboration with other businesses, often in different industries. Cross-industry collaboration, which requires workers with creative, organizational, and communication skills, will define future business. Such a circular economy is essential.

It is time to separate economic health from economic growth—at least the kind of growth that requires ever-increasing extraction of natural resources. It is not pie in the sky to say so. Germany, Japan, and China, among other governments, have made it their policy to create circular economies that promote reduction, reuse, and recycling of materials.

The United States needs to build its own circular economy. This would require eliminating government subsidies and tax breaks for industrial agriculture as well as oil and gas production and other nonrenewable resources, so that prices would reflect true costs. The US Treasury, for example, pays $2 billion a year to support the price of chemically intensive conventional cotton grown in California and Texas. What if the Treasury moved that subsidy to regenerative agriculture to support growing food that's good for people and the planet?

In the coming decades as customers become more insistent on companies being responsible, environmental laws (we hope) become more restrictive, resources become less plentiful and more costly, and more investors demand sustainability, companies will face competitors who embrace all the elements of business responsibility—not always because it's the right thing to do, but because it is essential to their success. Eventually, the business world will recognize the economic and environmental equivalent of the astronomic truth that the Earth rotates around the sun, not the other way around. Our economy revolves around nature, not the other way around. As we destroy nature, so we destroy our economy.

## Responsibility to Society

A company can do many things right for these five stakeholders and, alas, still be irresponsible. Imagine a business that returns a tidy profit, treats its employees well, makes the best-quality product possible, gives generously to the community, rebuilds its headquarters to LEED or Living Building standards and throws in a rooftop garden— but makes land mines. The company doesn't make them in the United States, where it has been illegal to make land mines since 1997, but offshore, through its supply chain.

Many companies, some highly admired in the pages of business journals and on Wall Street, make things like cigarettes, the Cadillac Escalade, Lucky Charms, hollow-point bullets, baby toys containing endocrine-disrupting phthalates, and lead-containing lipstick. Some behave responsibly in important ways, then hire teams of lobbyists to promote the good they do and discredit the worthy science that exposes the wrongs. These companies export dirty products (toxic food, cosmetics, chemicals) banned by the European Union to other countries that still allow them. But it's not enough for companies to argue that they're simply meeting customer demand where it's legal to do so. The Sackler family donated significant sums to the arts even as they made and dishonestly marketed OxyContin as not addictive. They can't repay the damage done through philanthropy. If you make a bad product or sell a risky one, regardless of your good actions or policies, it's bad business.

# 4
# What to Do?

"Know your impacts, favor improvement, share what you learn," says science writer Daniel Goleman. These rules to reduce environmental harm apply to us all, in large and small companies, as we begin or continue to act. As a method, they work in sequence: You have to know your adverse impacts before you can favor improvements, before you can share what you've learned.

What follows are practical questions and tips for companies getting started on the journey. We include, as an appendix, a checklist of responsible practices a company can undertake in relation to each of its stakeholders. The checklist is meant to be used as a handy cross-reference with this chapter.

For a more comprehensive self-examination, we strongly recommend you take the B Impact Assessment (https://www.bcorporation.net/en-us/programs-and-tools/b-impact-assessment). More than 150,000 companies have already done so, many as a first step toward becoming a B Corp. The website will take you through the process of self-assessment, help you compare your performance against that of other companies, and suggest processes for making improvements.

## Where to Start?

Deciding what to tackle first is never easy, but try applying the 80/20 rule. If 20 percent of your products (or services) generate 80 percent of your sales, analyzing those products will gauge the lion's share of

GIOTEX Sustainable Textiles in Mérida, Yucatán, Mexico, recycles
fabric scraps into cotton yarn for Patagonia.  KERI OBERLY

your impact. As we mentioned, 97 percent of Patagonia's impact is in our supply chain. Companies with deep supply chains like ours have to really dig to learn all that goes on in our name. It's useful to remember that 90 percent of a product's environmental impact is determined at the design stage. All the improvements you make start with the designer considering product quality, including its social and environmental performance, and its ability to be repaired, reused, and ultimately recycled.

## What Kind of Business Are You?

Companies that make things, or cause things to be made, have especially significant responsibilities. Pay special attention to the environmental section of the checklist in the appendix.

Are you a service provider? If so, you are seriously responsible to a community—or multiple kinds of communities. See the community checklist.

## What Is Your Role in Your Company?

If you're not the owner or the CEO or you don't have the power to establish a "corporate sustainability program," start anywhere. Scan the checklist to see what you, in your role, can do. It is a myth that taking better care of people and nature is at odds with business excellence. But what if your boss believes that? Concentrate on money-saving steps that also save the planet. No boss worth her stock options will stop you from saving the company money.

Say you are a CEO of a privately held business. You're committed; so is your company. You do have the power and you're ready to begin a material assessment of your impact. Take the B Impact Assessment to evaluate how your actions affect each of your stakeholders. If you have a deep supply chain, investigate the Higg

Index for help with a material assessment of the 20 percent of your activities that generate 80 percent of your negative social and environmental footprint.

Say you're the CEO of a publicly traded company. You're not committed but would like to go green—or at least greener. You don't have the power others might think you have. You answer to a board and have to appease nervous stockholders whose politics and environmental knowledge vary; you work in a volatile stock-centric business climate that muddles every tealeaf used for forecasting. You might have to rely on a chief financial officer or chief operating officer who is still convinced that climate change is a hoax. How do you get them going? How do you bring your people along?

As a CEO of any company experimenting with change, you can undertake greening in three steps.

1. Engage your team, with as broad a participation as possible, to find out the worst things your company does, what costs you the most in reputation and profit, and what will be the easiest problem to correct. The easiest problems for your company to correct may seem complex and difficult to another. The ease or difficulty of any greening endeavor depends on a business's values and operational strengths.

Address first what you already suspect; tease it out. What nags at you most whenever you hear about it (or see its consequences)? What do you think you can do something about that your company will be good at getting done? Ask your team to ask themselves the same questions. And ask them to ask their teams the same questions. The air can get cloudy at the top and obscure conditions on the ground.

2. Get together with your team to name priorities for improvement based on your assessment, then winnow the list. Decide with your team what you'll do first, how much time and money you'll spend on it, and how many people will be involved. Define what initial success will look like. Condense that vision into one page that you can circulate among your direct reports. Once you've figured out what

improvements you want to make and where you can draw on your company's greatest strengths, take the fewest risks, save the most money, and create the most opportunity, go for it.

As you learn what works and what doesn't, share your lessons with as many people as possible in your organization, even if you don't think you (or they) have the time. Then share what you learn with stakeholders: suppliers, trade association, key customers, even the key competitors you call on when you need to form a united front to get something done. Telling the same story of your intentions, successes, and failures to each of your stakeholders will earn their trust. That, in turn, creates a little snowball of support.

3. Finally, using the trust you've deepened, the knowledge you've gained, and the confidence and pride that have grown throughout the organization and among your stakeholders, ask yourself: What does your company now know that enables you to take the next step that may have been out of reach before, but suddenly is within sight?

Are (or were) you a juvenile delinquent? Great. You have the personality of an entrepreneur. Read all the checklists and go do something that makes you proud.

## Keep Going. Here's What Will Happen.

The company will get smarter, and more people will start to care deeply about raising the quality of the company through improving its social and environmental performance. Now your team will *have* to pay better attention to all the business fundamentals, and this boost in applied intelligence will result in a more fluid, less wasteful organization. You will spot money leaks you could not see before because your people know it will make a difference if they point them out. You will start to recognize problems and pursue opportunities that a company bound by traditional corporate see-no-evil politesse cannot even envision. Success motivates people, even your strays. Redefine success as not only a stronger balance sheet but greener, more humane operations. These goals are mutually reinforcing, not mutually exclusive.

Doing Good Creates Better Business.

We know this from experience, from our own years in business and from talking to other businesspeople. Unilever, a consumer-products giant, recently found that half its growth and half its profits arose from its forty (out of 400) most socially and environmentally conscious brands.

Expect internal resistance at first, depending on what you try to do. The poet William Stafford once wrote that no poem should begin with a first line the reader can argue with. Get your people nodding in full agreement a few times before you say something that challenges the half-sleep of received wisdom.

You might start a social and environmental initiative with something relatively obvious that unarguably needs doing. As they gain experience, your colleagues will become more aware of the nuanced, harder-to-spot social and environmental impacts, and of opportunities to reduce them. They will start to share a language of and cultural bias toward improvement. Managers often cling to the safety of familiar practices until they see their colleagues (and competitors within the company) dare to imagine and then implement better practices. Courage can be contagious. So is success.

You'll need the support, early on, of company heroes at various levels in the hierarchy who are respected for their wisdom or competence or both. These heroes may not be among the company's most predictable social and environmental advocates; they might not sing in the progressive choir. Expect and welcome surprising sources of collaboration, especially from thoughtful, religiously motivated or stewardship-inspired conservatives. Expect the collaborative process to change the company and everyone involved.

Share what you learn as often and with as many people as you can. Transparency will gradually increase your base of committed support within the company, from the margins (or the heights) to the center; entrenched traditionalists gradually shuffle to the side, go elsewhere, or retire.

As your employees learn more and gain the confidence to work cooperatively with colleagues inside and outside the company to improve environmental and social performance, they will adopt that work permanently as *part of their job*. It becomes irresistible. The work becomes unstoppable.

Eventually, this sends the siloed walls of Jericho tumbling down. That has been our experience at Patagonia, which once had three big subcultures—bean counters, go-getter product champions, and tree huggers—competing for the soul (and pocketbook) of the company. No one ever won. Instead, the culture as a whole advanced. Everything began to change in a way no one really noticed at first. There were no more arguments about the need to balance purpose and profit. It dawned on us that our purpose was now driving the business model. There was no separation. The constraints we placed on ourselves had forced us to stay awake and innovate when most companies pursued ruthless—relatively mindless—efficiency, reducing costs year by year until the world moved on. We found the world moving our way. Innovation led to new and better products.

The go-getter product champions still want to increase their sales and market share and keep margins in line. Success means increasing sales *and* solving environmental problems. At Patagonia, an alpine line manager knows she must also place more of her products in Fair Trade Certified factories and find a replacement for the water repellent made of toxic chemicals that persist in the atmosphere. She and her team feel ownership of that responsibility.

Our bean counters have gone solidly green. They're doing business, as much as possible, with banks and insurance companies that are helping the transition from fossil fuels to clean energy. Our financial and operations teams made the decision on their own to site our East Coast distribution center on the reclaimed surface of a coal mine rather than plow up raw farmland or forests. They needed no guidance from a "corporate sustainability team."

So, you're not a CEO. Most consultants and experts we know argue that any major social and environmental initiative must come from the top down, from the leadership. Of course, no formal company initiative can succeed without top-down support or at least benign neglect. Nevertheless—and your CEO likely does not believe this—most fundamental changes of any kind start on the ground and

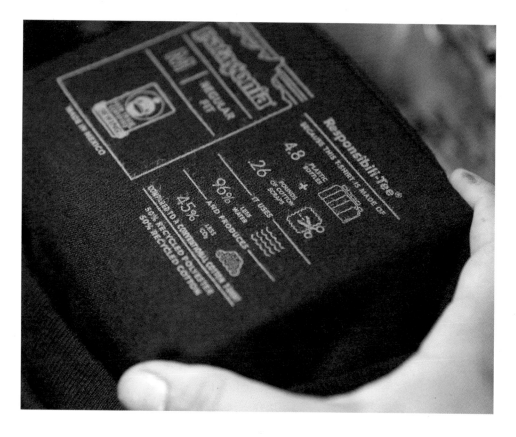

Vertical Knits, in Baca, Yucatán, Mexico, produces Responsibili-Tee® shirts for Patagonia. KERI OBERLY

move toward the center and up. As long as reducing environmental harm presents so many opportunities for companies to save or make money—and it does—you can't go wrong pursuing improvements from the bottom up.

It's always easiest to start with what can be done least expensively (or produces the most savings), and with the least resistance. But also look at what seems most difficult and far-fetched. What seems hardest, or boldest, to do may be precisely what you need to do to motivate others, including customers and competitors, as well as suppliers, to join you in your efforts. Checking off the easy stuff gives us experience and builds confidence. Tackling the big stuff, and surviving setbacks and failures, makes us smarter, stronger, and more useful to others. Doing both can lead to environmental and social gains of the sort we need: some wildly imaginative, some quietly effective.

It will take all kinds of companies and businesspeople to repair the damage we've done to our planet. And all kinds of stories to effect change. Nissan heroically kept its electric car, the LEAF, in production early in the twenty-first century in the face of a tepid response from the automotive world and dispiriting sales. Nissan's advertising had the usual Birkenstock-and-granola colors that marketers assign to the sustainable. Then along came the Tesla S, named by *The Wall Street Journal*'s automotive reporter as the best car ever made. The entire electric car industry benefited from the boost and learned that sustainable-minded people are not limited in their taste to beige and brown.

## Can We Boil This Down?

We go back to Daniel Goleman's creed: Know your impacts, favor improvement, and share what you learn.

Doing the right thing usually gives people courage to do more of the right thing. Companies that recognize the opportunity to use the intelligence and creative capacity of their people to do less harm will benefit. The company that commits less environmental destruction will simultaneously reduce its sharply rising costs for energy, water, and waste disposal.

Smaller companies can latch onto the efforts of bigger companies and dare to do what larger companies may not be limber enough to do. Bigger companies can accomplish big things; harm done on an industrial scale needs to be reduced on an industrial scale.

We advocate a combination of steady improvements with the occasional, breathtakingly bold move to keep everyone awake and motivated, and to demonstrate leadership that reflects well on the whole company. Bold moves that disrupt accepted practices often lead to the discovery of a new, more responsible product or service.

No one needs to sit out the dance. Even if you work in an apathetic company, ask yourself, what are my social and environmental responsibilities and possibilities here? Do the best you can to act on them.

The environmental crisis has arrived in tandem with a crisis of labor. The advanced industrial economies no longer create enough well-paying jobs; the job base no longer underpins the economy with any stability. We need a new economy, or more of this economy, built on smaller-scale enterprise that is more attentively and responsibly managed. And we have no time to lose.

How will you know if you're on track? Over time, your company will become healthier as a benefit of knowing your business more intimately, and more fully engaging your workforce and community. You'll know you're on track whenever you ask yourself and your colleagues, why didn't we do this sooner?

# 5
# Sharing What You Learn

When employees perceive a company strategy that lacks integrity—is not grounded in its purpose, capabilities, or reality—they call bullshit. That is, if you're lucky. Workers who don't believe in a company's strategy often sabotage it, not defiantly but by quietly ignoring it as they go about their daily work. As attributed to management guru Peter Drucker, "Culture eats strategy for breakfast."

The strategy of environmental and social improvement is too critical to be ignored and too complex to be mandated from above without the commitment of the company's whole culture. At this juncture, the work to reverse nature's decline is so new, it needs to be shared, so we novices can learn from one another.

We struggled for years to develop an honest, hard look at our own practices that we could share with the public. When we created Our Footprint, we intended it as an interactive website for graduate students, NGOs, and the nerdiest of customers who wanted to learn about the creation of Patagonia products from the oil well or farm to manufacturing and shipping to our warehouse. We were surprised by the strong response from two unexpected constituencies. First, our employees, who became, through learning more about what they made, smarter and more cooperative. Our Footprint improved the quality of debate within the company about our social and environmental practices. The watercooler conversations became more serious and less snarky. We became more capable of solving problems together.

Our Footprint's effect on our suppliers also surprised us. Arvind, a large vertical supplier in India, contracts with cooperatives of

A Fair Trade Certified™ information display at the Patagonia
Santa Monica store, California. KENNA REYNER

organic-cotton farmers to spin and sew the cotton into jeans in Arvind's factories. We currently work with them on our pilot program for regenerative organic cotton. But when we started with Arvind fifteen years ago, we violated one of our own rules: to visit a factory to do a social audit before we place the first order. We had our excuses: Our director of social responsibility had left the company, our new director had not yet arrived, and Arvind had an excellent reputation. So, we punted. When our new director made the trip after production had begun, she found several violations of our Code of Conduct, some small, some major, some cultural: flip-flops worn around chemicals, no railing around a wastewater pool, a first-aid cabinet locked to prevent theft. We met with Arvind managers and said we wanted to discuss this visit on our website and work with them to resolve the violations. The conversations were difficult but, to their credit, they agreed. The open discussion of problems and their resolution earned Arvind some new customers who were impressed more by their transparency than by ours. Soon some of our other suppliers wanted to be chronicled as well.

Every responsible company must involve outsiders in its quest to share information with—and tap information from—suppliers, customers, competitors, standards-setting organizations, independent monitors, and so on. Companies rightly guard certain information, like patentable technology, business-development strategy, the mysterious Madagascar source for the vanilla in the cookie batter. Much of what companies hold secret, however, would be better off revealed. Your factory list? Publish it. This lends your competitors, who may be less bold than you, a new, adoptable "best practice." The more you reveal about your challenges and successes, the more you help others in your industry who are trying to reduce their social and environmental footprint. When it comes to protecting nature and human beings from harm, we are all on the same side.

It makes sense, moreover, for companies to organize themselves into industry-wide working groups to develop a shared methodology

NEXT SPREAD More patches than pockets:
Kevin Prince's hand-me-down serves him well
in Patagonia, Argentina. AUSTIN SIADAK

SHARING WHAT YOU LEARN

to address, say, materials shortages, emissions, and effluents, and the need for a better grievance process for workers on the floor. Collaborative colleagues can establish agreed-upon group standards for animal welfare, chemical use, product quality, and labor practices. We have been active as founding members of the Fair Labor Association, Textile Exchange, and Sustainable Apparel Coalition, and we've been closely involved with the Outdoor Industry Association, B Lab, and Bluesign. This kind of industry-shifting cooperation cannot happen without transparency.

There are limitations to all reporting methods; we are all still finding our way, but we're now building on two decades of work. Accountability is especially limited, of course, when performance is self-reported and there is no independent oversight. Companies can manipulate the numbers to improve their score for a certification at the expense of actual performance.

Patagonia makes it a point to rely on independent oversight as well as self-reporting. Sometimes the self-reporting has been painful, especially about problems that at first seemed beyond our control. We collectively groaned when we learned how harmful conventionally grown cotton was. We groaned louder when we began to understand how much work would be involved in a switch to organic cotton.

When we agreed to become a member of President Clinton's task force on sweatshop labor, we didn't really know if we were in the clear ourselves. We wiped the fog from our lens only with the help of the Fair Labor Association, the independent verification service that grew out of the task force. We couldn't do everything alone. No one can.

Sometimes what we need to know about ourselves is beyond us. Even though we have textile scientists on staff, we do not have even close to the necessary knowledge of chemicals and toxins to conduct our own audits of dyehouses and fiber manufacturers. It has been invaluable to team with Bluesign Technologies, which does have the necessary expertise to assess our suppliers' use of chemicals.

Our transparency illustrates the seriousness of our standards to our suppliers. It has improved the quality of our clothing to have it sewn by people who are decently treated by managers held accountable for their behavior. By examining our supply chain, we got to know our suppliers better. Because we learned what our suppliers do, how they do it, and the specific challenges of their work, they trust us more. We can solve problems of any kind with them more quickly.

With customers, there are two strong trends at cross-purposes. There are those who buy from Amazon, and to a lesser extent Walmart and Costco and other big-box stores, who care mostly about convenience and low price, or a combination of the two. And there are those who, though they may also buy a book or toothbrush from Amazon, buy fewer, better-made things that will last longer and perform better than what you can buy on the cheap. Many of these customers who care more about the quality of what they buy also care about how it's made and by whom, and under what conditions. Your transparency earns their loyalty. The knowledge you share also informs customers who have been drawn to products for their cheap price what the true costs are and why, even on a tight budget, they should prefer healthful food over fast food or durable clothes over fast fashion.

Transparency is a precondition of positive change but does not guarantee it. Years ago, we developed a group of durable new day-packs. They sold well. Yet we knew we had cut environmental corners to shave cost to meet the price we thought would generate strong sales and sufficient profit. We used no recycled fabrics in these packs, as had been our custom. So, we said all this on our website. The result? No customers complained, sales remained brisk, and our designers, though ashamed of themselves, failed to come up with a more environmentally friendly fabric that performed equally well. Transparency may hold feet to the fire but doesn't always toast the soles; shame doesn't always change behavior. In our experience, though, often sharing what you learn inspires and facilitates change.

For the responsible company, then, strategy starts with the real story. To be credible—and relatable—a company's story includes its virtues and vices, its strengths and weaknesses, as well as its aspirations. It must resonate with your employees' perceptions of the company and their role in it. To be credible, the story you tell your employees should be roughly the same one you tell your banker, your customers, your suppliers, and the community at large. When your stories align, your stakeholders believe you. Your business strategy becomes something nobody wants to ignore.

# 6

# Making a Living in the Anthropocene

Younger people sometimes approach us for career advice, which we're reluctant to give. We know only one company well, and we rarely know the advice seekers well enough to understand their strengths and motivations. Advice we can give: Explore what kind of work the world needs now.

We've looked at what makes work meaningful for individuals and why meaningful work motivates us. But what kind of work will be most effective to slow, and then reverse, the destruction of the planet's life zone? What jobs will restore the Earth and its oceans and strengthen human society? For those who want to have a good life and do good work, where are the opportunities?

What follows is our sense of the work to be done that will generate great companies and a useful living for many. Much of the work is in new fields not yet broadly known, offering jobs not fully defined but steadily taking shape.

We'll start in the more familiar spots, then head off into the ultima Thule—the land beyond the borders of the known world—of a new economy.

## Holding Feet to the Fire: Policy Work

Treaties with more good intentions than teeth can be dismissed, like hypocrisy itself, as the homage vice pays to virtue. But when agreed to by more than 95 percent of the world's 195 nations, treaties

Barnacle Foods uses Alaskan kelp to make foods that benefit coastal and Indigenous communities while providing a low-carbon input food source. BETHANY SONSINI GOODRICH do change the way governments and business elites think and plan—and act. Even as the work goes too slowly, the common language and framing of the Paris Agreement and the UN Sustainable Development Goals (SDGs) represent significant wins. The handwringing question of "what is to be done" has been negotiated and settled.

The seventeen SDGs are almost ludicrously aspirational, among them: end poverty in all its forms, ensure clean water and energy, make cities livable and inclusive, and change the patterns of consumption that are the root cause of climate change, biodiversity loss, and pollution. Do not dismiss these goals for the scale of their ambition; this is the work that needs to be done.

A third major treaty will provide new opportunities in the decade ahead. In 2022, 190 national governments formally signed onto the 30×30 Initiative. (The United States is not party to the treaty due to opposition in the Senate, but the Biden administration has issued an executive order to implement its own 30×30 plan.) Restoration ecology is critical to our future. Nature, when allowed, comes back. There is work to be done to support the Earth's efforts.

We have learned at Patagonia that big, lofty goals can be more than slogans etched on a plaque and forgotten. Our collective clarity of purpose, articulated in our original mission statement, helped shape our actions for almost fifty years, just as our new statement will shape what we do going forward. The companies, governments, and civic organizations of the future will need workers to conceive, write, and defend environmental treaties, legislation, corporate governance rules, statements of purpose, and contracts. Students of urban planning, engineering, law, public health, Earth science, architecture, environmental studies, ecology, theology, philosophy, and business would do well to consider careers in policy to advance the adoption and realization of ambitious agreements to restore the health of our home planet.

Helping Carbon Get Back to Where It Belongs:
Drawdown

The aim of the 2017 book *Drawdown*, edited by Paul Hawken, was to
lay out a comprehensive plan to displace enough carbon emissions
by 2050 to prevent a rise of more than two degrees Celsius in global
temperature. Its authors evaluated eighty innovations and practices
that will help draw carbon back into the ground. All of them are well
beyond prototype stage. Some are social—for example, the universal
education of girls and family planning is high on the list. Most relate
to energy and agriculture. Recommendations include onshore wind
farms and rooftop solar. Agricultural recommendations include
reducing food waste, plant-rich diets, tropical forest protection, and
silvopasture (the integration of grazing livestock and forests). Many
recommendations for sinking carbon have knock-on benefits: They
can also stem or slow the loss of habitat and species. For those who
want to do useful work, *Drawdown* is a good survey of what's both
necessary and feasible.

Electrifying the Economy

Electrification of the economy is well underway, though the challenge
of storage remains. Meeting this challenge is key to planetary survival because electricity can then be derived entirely from renewable
energy rather than fossil fuels. Energy from solar and wind is now
cheaper to produce than using coal—and a third cheaper even than
natural gas. Those who resist the transition can no longer credibly
argue that renewables are too expensive and unreliable.

In California, new homes must be wired for all-electric heating
and appliances, and new buildings of three stories or less must have
rooftop solar. The sale of new gas furnaces and water heaters will
be banned in the state by 2030. Throughout the developed world,

Interns harvesting Kernza for The Land Institute, Salina, Kansas.
AMY KUMLER

municipalities, regulators, and energy companies are closing or phasing out coal plants. You can buy electric vehicle chargers online and find them at more and more gas stations and parking lots.

Not to paint too rosy a picture: Coal is a still a major source of energy for China and India—and the United States as well. Even in Europe, coal consumption increased 20 percent at the outset of Russia's invasion of Ukraine to offset reduced availability of Russian gas. India recently reopened 100 coal mines to meet the demand for electricity in response to heat waves of unprecedented intensity and duration. It's still a race to move to renewable energy before fossil fuels warm the planet past the tipping point.

But the race is very much on. There is good work to be done by myriad new businesses during the transition—and now, because of demonstrated economic feasibility, there is far more money available to finance it. There will also be policymaking needed to help order and speed the transition, beginning with closing the pipelines of the worst fossil fuels as quickly as possible, namely, coal and tar sands.

## Enriching the Soil

People need a new jacket every five or ten years, but we eat three times a day. Saving our planet starts with food, and food starts with soil. If we kill off our soil we're done for. If we nurture it without chemicals and honor its genetic richness as a source of life, we start to save our home planet.

Anyone who has tasted a carrot from a home garden or an organic farmers market knows the difference soil makes in the quality of food and the quality of life. Regenerative organic agriculture builds topsoil far faster than nature can unassisted, and as we have mentioned, it holds the potential to bolster place-based conservation and revive rural communities that have been gutted by industrial agriculture and its absentee corporate owners. Regenerative practices suit

smallholder farming: Minimal tillage, crop rotation, and companion planting all require closer attention from a farmer than using
Roundup on a monocultural scale.

Regenerative organic agriculture represents our best future, but
its adoption, unlike that of renewable energy, is in the earliest stages.
Not surprisingly, agribusiness and the chemical industry have promoted the use of chemicals for low-tillage "regenerative agriculture"
and left "organic" behind.

America's smallholder farmers could work together to create a new
self-sustaining business network parallel to monocultural, chemical-
intensive Big Ag, which will eventually displace it. Start with innova-
tive distribution schemes that circumvent long-distance truck travel
in favor of farmers markets and neighborhood delivery.

For those who don't want to spend their lives in front of a screen
and do want to engage nature in all its richness, go for it: Farm a patch
of land and sell what you grow. Want to learn how to get started? The
Market Gardener Institute, founded by Jean-Martin Fortier and
Suleyka Montpetit, hosts online classes in small-scale regenerative
organic farming. On his website, Charles Dowding teaches a "no dig"
method that builds soil health and improves yields.

## Making Peace Between Town and Country

In many developing countries, small-scale farming is viewed by elites
as a gateway to the past. Elites in developed countries tend to view
any small-scale business as a boutique concern to be absorbed by the
universal drive to grow big. We think the opposite. Small-scale enterprises, including farming, make possible a more promising future for
human and planetary health.

The social benefits of "small" can be big, indeed, when enterprises
organize themselves cooperatively with the well-being of workers
and the community in mind. The global success of the fair-trade

Natural latex, the base material for our wetsuits, flows from a Hevea tree in the highlands of Guatemala. TIM DAVIS

movement provides a critical example. In general, citizens who share a watershed or beloved local forest have more incentive to solve their problems or disputes imaginatively, civilly, and with fewer resources than do anonymous virtual enemies pressing "Send" on the internet.

Rural residents in the United States without much money or advanced diplomas may tend to entrust their fate to the company providing the local jobs. They don't view it as within their power to restore their local waterways, forests, or soil—let alone address the challenges of a warming climate and rising seas. This sense of impotence and inertia can be reversed in communities where people sense their own agency in jobs that maintain, or at least take into consideration, the health of their home place.

We tend to associate endemic wisdom with Indigenous people who have been in a place for generations and whose traditions have been eclipsed by and conflict with modernity—and in so doing, we forget our own connection and responsibility to place. In fact, all rural people who farm, hunt, fish, build things, and raise animals and children have a visceral relationship to place and need to work together (regardless of, or better yet, taking advantage of their differences) to protect it.

The future health of both town and country relies on reducing the city's extractive economic power and preserving a rural area's sense of place. Hugo & Hoby's business model makes the point. Fred Kukelhaus and Ben Young, who began the company while roommates at graduate school, wanted to make high-quality, durable furniture with sustainable practices and to employ local artisans. Hugo & Hoby, named after their grandfathers, is a B Corp and a member of 1% for the Planet. It sources wood locally, using recycled and reclaimed materials where possible, and plants new trees in at-risk forests. The company is committed to manufacturing on a small scale in local workshops in rural New England, where Ben lives, and in the Southeast, near Fred. As they expanded and became more successful, Fred and

Ben increased the number of small workshops they employed rather than move the business to larger fabricators.

A healthy rural life is good for those who have it, and for those in the city nearby who rely on the countryside for water, food, and recreation. There is a need to innovate and develop smaller-scale American enterprises in the years ahead.

## Building a Circular Economy

How do we learn from nature to conserve resources, use the energy available to us, and generate no waste? Animal scat is plant food. Deadfall is habitat. Nature is a circular economy; ours needs to become circular, too.

The growing field of industrial ecology ascribes ecological thinking to industrial systems. Marian Chertow at the Yale School of the Environment has been a pioneer in industrial ecology and in the subfield of industrial symbiosis, which focuses on the sharing of resources by companies in relative proximity. Popularized by the Ellen MacArthur Foundation as the circular economy, industrial symbiosis is the grounding principle for business solutions to climate change, biodiversity loss, waste, and pollution. A thing should be made to last. Before it comes to the end of its useful life, recycle it into something new of the highest possible value; share, lease, sell, resell, repair, and reuse it. Patagonia's Worn Wear program reflects this principle.

Circularity has been endorsed or adopted by companies such as Ikea, Burger King, and Adidas; countries, including the Netherlands, France, China, and India; and government agencies, such as the American EPA and—surprise—the US Chamber of Commerce.

Some of the most interesting circular economy business is being done, as we shall see later in this chapter, by four companies in Halifax, Nova Scotia.

Living Systems

"Out of the crooked timber of humanity no straight thing was ever made," said Immanuel Kant, which is a lovely metaphor, but also a rudimentary lesson that nothing comes "straight" out of nature. As tool users, humans tend to make things straight so that the corners join perfectly, and the surface is level; our predilection for smoothing things out and making them uniform can hurt us when we try to solve existential problems. Things may be mechanical, but the world is organic, and harder to understand.

As we began to see earlier in the "Building a Circular Economy" section, we can learn from nature how to heal the damage we inflict. According to John Fullerton, any healthy political, financial, or industrial system shares eight principles with nature's living systems, among them: the ability to adapt to changing circumstances, "robust circulatory flow," and the tendency to be most creative and abundant at the edges.

A former investment banker dedicated to the transformation of our financial system, Fullerton uses the term *regenerative capitalism* to describe an economic model that uses circular (make, use, repair, recycle) rather than linear (make, use, dispose) systems as a model for business. Although still a hypothesis, his living-systems principles serve as a litmus test for the social success and ecological efficacy of an organization's actions.

Breaching the Boundaries of Living Systems

For those who want to make products or offer services that move us back from the edge of the precipice, it's useful to learn the nine planetary boundaries identified by the Stockholm Resilience Centre in 2009. These environmental thresholds that cannot be crossed without endangering life provide a framework for anyone launching

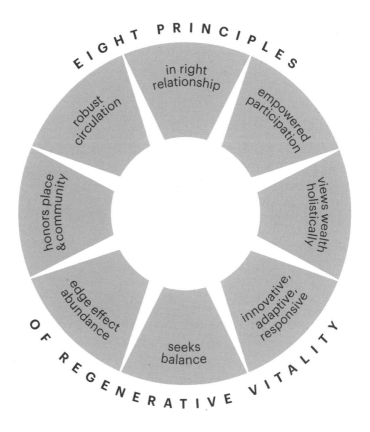

a company. The boundaries include climate change, ocean acidification, freshwater depletion, chemical pollution, and nitrogen and phosphorus flows from agriculture into the biosphere. For each boundary, the risk of crossing is defined as low, medium, or high.

Importantly, the Centre examines how the threats of climate change, biodiversity loss, and resource depletion interrelate. This helps us identify how existing products need to be changed to both reduce their overall impact and improve their performance. The planetary boundaries, individually and holistically, present a worthy challenge for businesses. For a single product, or in a single action, how many boundaries can we make more distant?

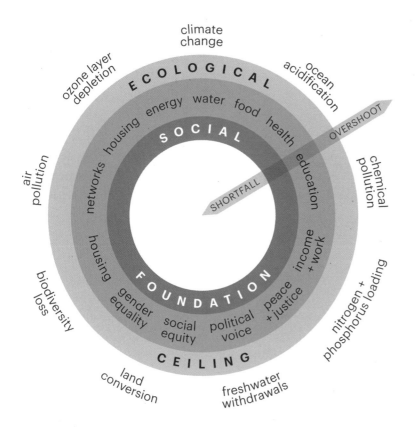

## Examining Doughnut Economics

Renegade economist Kate Raworth devised "Doughnut Economics" to add a social component to the planetary boundaries. The Doughnut recognizes ecological overshoot, but also social shortfall, where people live with hunger and need below the foundation that supports everyone else.

Doughnut Economics has appealed to localities confronting the degraded health of both the community and the environment. In 2019, the C40 Cities Climate Leadership Group, a global network of ninety-six

mayors focused on climate change, asked Raworth to use her framework to evaluate three of its members—Amsterdam, Portland, and
Philadelphia. How far outside the sweet spot did their people live?

The following year, during the COVID pandemic, Amsterdam
adopted the Doughnut, combined with a circular economy strategy, as its development model. The new thinking has manifested in
large ways and small. A new neighborhood under construction on
reclaimed land had its foundations laid so that sea level could safely
rise around it. Meanwhile, a city committee examining the effects of
social isolation during the COVID lockdown found that thousands of
residents had no access to a computer. Rather than buy new products,
they rounded up broken computers throughout the city, along with
unused spare parts, and hired a refurbishing firm that made 3,500
machines to alleviate people's isolation.

Other cities around the world have expressed interest, and citizens'
groups have lobbied their local governments to adopt the Doughnut
model. There is much to be done to encourage and activate this new way
of connecting the health of human community with the health of a place.

## Pursuing Reconciliation: Fish in the Field

Conservationist Huey Johnson, Yvon's mentor and good friend, wanted
to help end the practice of mining the oceans for meal of sardines, herring, and anchovies to feed chickens, pigs, and penned fish. He wondered whether fish meal could instead be sourced from domesticated
forage fish raised in the flooded rice fields in places like his home state
of California, as has been done in Asia for thousands of years.

Flooding the rice paddies in the fall was new for California farmers. Before the state strengthened its clean air laws, farmers would
burn off the straw after the fall harvest to prepare their fields for
seeding, creating a wall of smoke that extended to the Sierra mountains to the east. Once the new laws took effect, rice farmers flooded

their fields instead. An unexpected benefit was the resurgence of the Pacific Flyway, as millions of migratory birds flocked to the new source of water. Conservationists were delighted. The farmers, accidental environmental heroes, worked with scientists to vary the depth and timing of flooding over different fields to accommodate different bird species.

In a flooded field, however, the colonies of bacteria that consume the rice straw also excrete methane gas—a lot of it. Fallow rice fields contribute 12 percent of methane emissions, and methane itself comprises about 20 percent of total global greenhouse gas emissions. While less prevalent in the atmosphere than carbon dioxide, methane is more deadly. But nature has its own way to reduce the generation of methane in rice paddies around the world: phytoplankton that can consume methane-excreting bacteria and reduce their population. Unfortunately, they are in turn overpowered by predatory zooplankton. Forage fish, however, feast on zooplankton, allowing the phytoplankton to do their methane-removal work. The introduction of forage fish into low-oxygen water could reduce its methane emissions by 90 percent.

In 2016, Huey's Resource Renewal Institute introduced 45,000 Arkansas golden shiners to the Sacramento River Delta to great success. This resilient minnow thrived on the zooplankton, leaving enough bacteria-munching phytoplankton alive to reduce methane gas emissions by nearly two-thirds.

There were multiple gains. Newly introduced fish feces eliminated the need for liquid nitrogen fertilizer. When the fields are drained, the minnows can be harvested for use as bait or feed for poultry or pets, or as fertilizer. Harvesting farmed forage fish could reduce market pressure to take the ocean's stocks of sardines, anchovies, herring, and mackerel.

Harvesting forage fish also supplements a rice farmer's income. The California experiment provided evidence for expanding the ancient Asian practice of rice-fish farming.

Patagonia Provisions has become interested in the pacu, a forage fish introduced in the rice fields of Corrientes province, Argentina. The pacu, cousin to the fearsome piranha, has humanoid teeth shaped for eating seeds and nuts rather than jagged teeth to tear into flesh. It is a delicious, meaty fish that can grow to nearly ninety pounds—pacu short ribs are a delicacy. Patagonia Provisions will soon be offering rice from the Corrientes wetlands—and making use of the pacu in interesting new ways.

Introducing fish to the rice fields is a perfect example of "reconciliation ecology," in which working land is used to support other species while meeting human needs. This principle, in conjunction with the restoration ecology goals of 30×30, is critical to healing the planet. Reconciliation creates business opportunities to help save the planet, as we shall see in Halifax.

## The Halifax Model

Four companies work together in the Halifax area as a circular micro-economy, where one company's waste becomes another's feedstock. The collaborative efforts of these four firms—Sustainable Blue, Oberland Agriscience, Sustane Chester, and Smallfood—exemplify the principles of living systems, industrial ecology and symbiosis, living within planetary means, a community-based circular economy, and reconciliation ecology. Rick Koe, the venture capitalist–turned–entrepreneurial environmentalist, spearheaded the project, enlisting private investors, including Yvon. The Halifax model represents the potential to recycle 90 percent of a municipality's solid waste, generate natural fertilizer and feed that neutralizes toxic pollutants, and feed a world population that's still growing. It could also eliminate the horrors of open-net-pen fish farms.

As an angler, Yvon has long been dismayed by the dangers of open-net-pen salmon farming. The irony is that salmon farming once

represented hope for the species. Challenged by ecosystem deteri-
oration, wild stocks—especially of Atlantic salmon—started to lose
population in the 1960s. During the next decade, small-scale open-
net-pen salmon farmers in Norway aimed to make up for the loss.
The business proved too expensive for them but lucrative for large
operators that bought up the leases abandoned by the locals. Farmed
salmon quickly became abundant and cheap—and big business in
Norway, Chile, Canada, and the United Kingdom.

But the drawbacks soon became apparent as the farms scaled into
operations holding as many as 200,000 fish in their cages. Crowded
into waters polluted by their own feces, suffering diseases caused by
that overcrowding, and infested with sea lice that attack their heads
and necks, caged salmon do not live a good life. Hormones accelerate
their growth at a speed their metabolism can't handle, and half are
deaf from deformed ears. Others suffer deformed spines, open sores,
and blisters. Antibiotics and antiviral pharmaceuticals are universally used, and their cost can exceed that of feed. Many of the fish
are sluggish and depressed. Some escape and spread sea lice to and
interbreed with wild salmon, weakening the species' ability to survive
the rigors of life in the open ocean and the return upriver against the
current to spawn. Escapees can be found in 87 percent of the rivers
within a three-hour drive of a fish farm.

The dangers are now generally recognized. Open-net-pen salmon
farms have been banned on the West Coast of the United States; a ban
is being considered in British Columbia. But there are still a number
of farms in the northeastern United States and Canadian Maritimes,
where tidal action generates enough oxygen to support farms of
enormous size.

*Sustainable Blue*
In Centre Burlington, Nova Scotia, situated on the Bay of Fundy an
hour's drive from Halifax, Sustainable Blue, a land-based salmon

farm, gains no advantage from the local forty-foot tides. Its salmon live out their lives on land in continuously filtered and recirculating water that is never released into an ocean, stream, or municipal water system. Nor is the system's solid waste released. Fish poop is filtered out, taken to a methane digester, and converted into electricity.

Kirk Havercroft, a native of the United Kingdom, runs Sustainable Blue. He worked for a dozen years with the company's founder, Dr. Jeremy Lee, to engineer the necessary equipment before beginning commercial operations. It took them another fifteen years to develop the Centre Burlington operation to an economically feasible scale.

Sustainable Blue's self-contained recirculating systems mimic the currents of the river and the sea. The fry start their life in fresh water and then graduate to larger, saltwater tanks. No growth hormones are introduced, no antibiotics. There are no sea lice. The saltwater tanks mimic ocean conditions and currents, so the salmon grow to adulthood lean, strong, and active. Sustainable Blue's harvested salmon have the full flavor and texture of wild salmon.

Many people around the globe rely on the oceans as their primary source of protein, but stocks of large fish have fallen precipitously during the past sixty years. Farming salmon responsibly could reduce damage to coastal waters and allow the revival of wild stocks while providing an efficient source of protein—and high-quality food.

A key element to Sustainable Blue's success is the quality and productivity of the feed. The company works with scientists at Dalhousie University who use artificial intelligence to calibrate the optimal mix. Wild-salmon fry eat insects primarily, and adults eat smaller fish. Penned salmon, whether fry or adult, are fed mixtures of soy and fish meal (from wild forage fish like anchovies and sardines). Salmon can consume more protein per weight than they generate. Sustainable Blue intends to improve the feed conversion ratio, increase growth rates without harming the fish, and reduce waste, and they are continuously refining their work. So far, Dalhousie researchers have developed a feed that increases growth by 20 percent, with 75 percent less waste. The feed includes, among other things, an ingredient produced by Oberland Agriscience, the next entity in the Halifax model.

*Oberland Agriscience*

The mix of feed developed by the Dalhousie researchers includes pacu, our humanoid-toothed friend from Argentina, which imparts its omega-3 fatty acids. Another key ingredient is black soldier fly larvae produced in Halifax by Oberland Agriscience, the brainchild of former rocket scientist Dr. Greg Wanger. Soldier flies, so named for their propensity to stand at seeming attention, are a yet-unheralded wonder of nature—an excellent source of protein that dramatically increases resource productivity while reducing resource intensity. The soldier flies are fed spent organic brewery grains (obtained free from Sustane Chester, the third entity in the circular microeconomy) and supermarket vegetables past their sell date.

A space of about 15 square feet holds 60,000 adult flies. The eggs, starting life at less than a millimeter long, grow to 8,000 times that size in ten days. Oberland's facility, which is a little over 100,000 square feet, can produce the nutrient equivalent of 5,700 acres (9 square miles) of corn, using a tiny fraction of the water. The facility is also a low carbon emitter, powered half by wind and half by solar in a city that still derives half its electricity from coal.

Soldier flies carry no human-transmissible diseases and have the capacity to neutralize toxins they ingest. The fully grown larvae are dried and ground into a powder that looks like coffee grounds and contains 55 percent protein by weight. The powder is then blended to make feed for dogs, chickens, and salmon. (Dr. Wanger tried to add them as an ingredient in cookies for his family, but it was no go.)

Lobster fishermen in Eastern Canada, under pressure to stop using wild forage fish like herring, mackerel, or sardines for bait, have found that soldier fly larvae, with soldier-fly frass (or excrement)

Zero fish escapes, zero growth hormones, zero waste-water. Sustainable Blue's state-of-the-art, land-based fishery in Centre Burlington, Nova Scotia, Canada.
SUSTAINABLE BLUE

for use as a binder and pressed into a hockey-puck-like mold, makes superlative lobster bait. The demand from the lobster trade has up-ended and accelerated Oberland's expansion plans. They will need to open four more plants just to satisfy the needs.

*Sustane Chester*

Oberland's free feedstock—the brewery grains and wet garbage—comes from Sustane's municipal solid-waste-processing plant in nearby Chester, the third company in the model. The plant, strategically located next to the local landfill, serves a population of 150,000 and has an annual processing capacity of 70,000 tons, the equivalent of removing 15,000 cars from the road. Sustane can recover more than 90 percent of the solid waste that would ordinarily wind up in the landfill next door and repurpose it into biomass pellets, diesel fuel, and recyclable metals. Sustane converts sandwich wrap, which few recyclers will take, into liquid polyethylene ready for a new use of equal value.

In Canada, less than 9 percent of plastics are recycled: most end up in landfills; 58 percent of food is wasted, most at the production stage. Imagine if every landfill—or, in other parts of the world, every incinerator—had a Sustane to reduce local methane and carbon dioxide emissions and plastic pollution, displace virgin fossil fuel production, nearly eliminate waste leachates, and free landfill space for other uses.

Sustane achieved its reductions through advanced separation technology with an emphasis on creating brand-new end products—like biomass pellets clean enough to be sold to paper mills and power plants as a coal-displacing energy source.

*Smallfood*

Another part of the mix for Sustainable Blue's feed—along with pacu and black soldier fly larvae—is marine microalgae. Marc St-Onge, owner and founder of Smallfood, believes his company is the first in Canada to get an aquaculture license for a single-cell organism.

This microbe, the result of ten years' research on more than 20,000 microorganisms, is high in protein and the omega-3 DHA found in salmon and fish-oil supplements. Through biomass fermentation (the process used to make kimchi or yogurt) in large vertical tanks, the microbe grows proteins that can also be sold as omega-3 lipids and antioxidants in foods, beverages, and supplements.

Smallfood's microbe provides impressive levels of protein and nutrition while occupying almost no land, using little water, and displacing the waste and greenhouse gases generated in most food production. The microbe can be directly ingested as an ingredient in food for humans as well as pets, including vegan "seafood." It is ready to ship after a seven-day production cycle. Microbes can feed the planet.

+++

Each of these Halifax businesses represents a regenerative and circular economic future. Each transforms the other's waste into productive raw material. Together they present business in its best form and on its best behavior by developing products that address multiple challenges and produce myriad benefits. Every Thursday, with Rick Koe advising, the four Halifax businesses get together by phone to discuss problems, strategies, and new ways to collaborate to address climate change and to slow or reverse nature's decline. They all focus on the quality of their work as well as innovation.

Huey Johnson would be pleased to see how his dream of saving wild forage fish has turned into a new form of capitalism. Instead of competing with one another, each company is working together for the common good. It's also a model we must use to correct the damage we have done to our home planet.

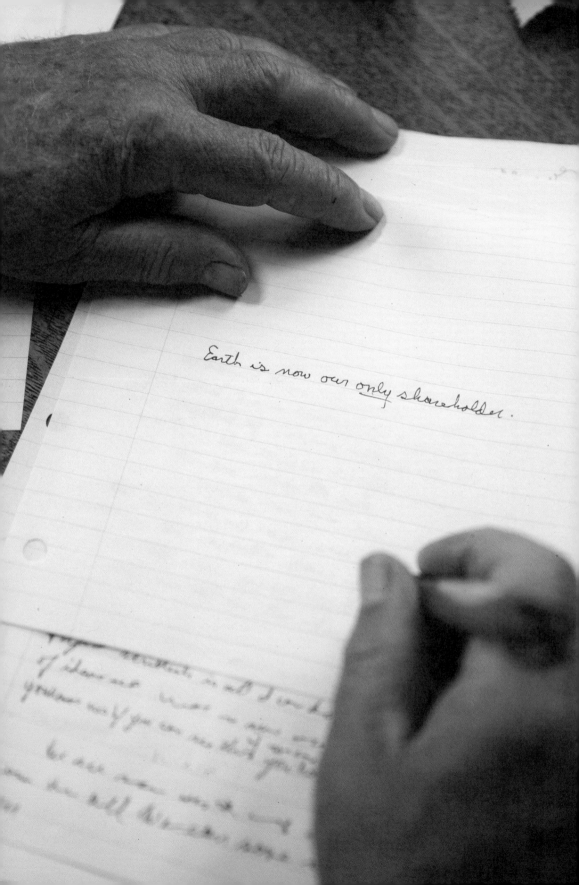

# 7

# What's Next for Patagonia?

"Every billionaire is a policy failure" is a bumper sticker Yvon liked well enough to put on his car. We both remember talks we had long ago on the way to visit an ailing friend about the need for Patagonia to be owned, ultimately, by a nonprofit, but that wasn't possible in the United States until 2018. With the recent shift from private ownership to the Patagonia Purpose Trust and the Holdfast Collective, the four adult members of the Chouinard family have happily found a way to stay this side of being a policy failure.

Patagonia remains a for-profit business, but its single shareholder is now the Earth or, to be precise, the benefit of the Earth. Patagonia will continue to reinvest a significant share of its profits back into the company each year and distribute another significant share of profits as bonuses to employees. The company will continue, through its Grants Council, to give its 1 percent of sales to grassroots environmental organizations. None of this will change.

What has changed is the structure of our company, which now aligns fully with its purpose. We hope others who have done well will see that they have enough for themselves and their families and follow suit.

Foundation-owned businesses, new to the United States, have been a feature of the northern European business landscape for more than a century. More than 50 percent of the German stock market value is in companies that have foundations as majority shareholders. Ikea, Rolex, and Heineken are owned by foundations. The Carl Zeiss Foundation has owned 100 percent of Carl Zeiss AG since 1889.

Our new structure doesn't ease the challenges we faced when we were family owned. With 97 percent of our environmental impact in the supply chain, most of it in the fabrics we use, we have much to do in the coming decades.

By the time you read this, Patagonia will have stopped, or nearly stopped, using newly drilled oil as feedstock for nylon and polyester, without sacrificing performance and durability. To forgo new oil in the making of synthetics puts to new use what is already made, for which the Earth has already literally paid a sunken cost.

The transformation of agriculture for fiber and food is as necessary as the greening of industry. By the end of the decade, we aim to switch to regenerative organic cotton and hemp for all our natural-fiber clothes, and in the process rebuild topsoil and sink carbon. For Patagonia Provisions, every new product, from the land or sea, must solve a problem in our food supply, as well as be nutritious and of superior quality. We will build awareness of the importance of small-scale farming and fishing, which needs financial, consumer, and political support.

The original customers of Chouinard Equipment for Alpinists were our friends, or friends of friends, who trusted their lives to the quality of our gear. We have always defined quality as durability, functionality, and as much versatility as possible. But quality in our age also means going beyond doing less harm to Mother Nature and actually returning the favor of her abundance. This means, ultimately, no pollution, no waste, no extraction in service to the pockets of the few at the expense of the many.

For the web of life to survive, we need to protect and restore vulnerable, degraded, and critically important land and water where we don't live, where the "hand of man does not linger" or where Indigenous communities have lived lightly for millennia. In the 2020s and 2030s, Patagonia will invest in activities that advance restoration ecology (giving nature the chance to revive), reconciliation ecology (letting nature thrive where we do our work), and the rewilding of species.

The work being done in Halifax is a far cry from how we operate at Patagonia, but we're paying attention to its lessons. This regenerative, circular, place-based effort represents the best possibilities for business as a social actor (along with civil society and government). Whether a business is owned by an individual, a family, a joint-stock company, or the Earth, it can, if it chooses, work in concert with all sectors of society in the interests of the common good and nature.

Patagonia will work with allies to support communities most impacted by environmental injustice. Chemical, oil, and gas plants are not built in Grosse Pointe or Marin County. They crop up where rents are cheap and voices are not heard—in Cancer Alley between Baton Rouge and New Orleans, or Chemical Alley along the Kanawha River in West Virginia, or in the neighborhoods next to the refineries of Richmond, California. In our state of California alone, people of color make up nearly 92 percent of the 1.8 million people living within a mile of oil and gas development, all at greater risk of chronic headaches, asthma, and cancer.

Nativists around the world displaced by the global economy, distrusting the institutions that failed them, have been courted by opportunist politicians with false promises of restored social status and security at the expense of immigrants and minorities. We need to support a politics and an economic vision that leave no one behind.

Patagonia, in this decade and those to come, is committed to democracy. This isn't nostalgia for what we learned in civics class but a necessity for saving ourselves and nature. The autocrats and plutocrats of the world will never work for harmony and justice that would put them out of business. As difficult as it is to identify common ground and cause, saving the home planet, place by place, is the work of us all.

+++

On September 14, 2022, local Patagonia colleagues and many invited former employees and friends gathered at our Brooks School campus in Ventura. Many other colleagues and friends from Reno and around the globe joined by video link. By then, we had all survived, like our readers, nearly three years of COVID, four years of Trump, and a decade of increasingly chaotic and deadly weather. For our local employees, the memory of the Thomas wildfire was still fresh, a symbol of the uncertainty inherent in our times. That day, in the Brooks garden, Malinda and Yvon Chouinard, and their adult children, Claire and Fletcher, announced that they no longer owned the company, they had given it to the Earth.

Cheryl Endo, a veteran employee who has long helped the design department keep operations on track, went up to our CEO, Ryan Gellert, and said, "I'm not taking any more of your guff." When Ryan looked puzzled, she added, pointing to a tall jacaranda nearby, "I don't work for you anymore. I work for that tree over there."

So should we all.

A day of joy and celebration, September 14, 2022, at Patagonia's Brooks campus, Ventura, California. NANCY PASTOR

# The Checklists

**Element #1:**
**Responsibility to Owners/Shareholders**

○ Maintain a board of directors that meets regularly, has at least one independent outside member, and oversees executive compensation.

○ Share financial information with all employees; no one should be uninformed.

○ Have financial controls in place to prevent fraud.

○ Have financial reports reviewed by the board of directors and audited by an independent accounting firm.

○ Incorporate into the purpose statement a commitment to reducing social and environmental harm. Share it with stakeholders.

○ Provide employee training to reduce social and environmental harm.

○ Dedicate staff, even if part-time, to monitor the company's social and environmental performance, preferably within operations.

PREVIOUS SPREAD Solar panels shade the parking lot and provide some power for Patagonia's main campus, Ventura, California. TIM DAVIS

NEXT SPREAD The Patagonia Santa Monica store front advocating for the local group STAND-L.A. in 2022, California. KENNA REYNER

## Element #2:
## Responsibility to Your Workers

○ Pay a living wage; if you can't, figure out when you can.

○ Determine whether your company pays above-market, at-market, or below-market rates. Paying below market means your competitors will attract the best talent, including yours.

○ Calculate the multiple by which the company's highest-paid employee compares to its lowest-paid full-time worker. Set a goal over a specific period to narrow the gap to a specific multiple.

○ Calculate your average annual attrition rate and compare it with that of other employers in your business. If your number doesn't look good, figure out why. Set a benchmark for improvement.

○ Calculate the internal hire rate for open positions. If you must hire outside too often, are you training properly and allowing people to grow in their jobs?

○ Distribute a portion of the company's annual profits to employees as a bonus. Include as many employees as possible in the company's bonus plan to secure broad-based support for company goals.

○ In the United States, offer health insurance to all half-time and full-time employees.

○ Make health insurance available at cost to employees' families and domestic partners. Offer flexible spending accounts (FSA).

○ Make available a 401(k) pension or equivalent plan for all employees after six months on the job.

STAND L.A.

STAND TOGETHER AGAINST

NEIGHBORHOOD OIL DRILLING

patago

Stand L.A.

OUR COMMUNITIES DESERVE

A CLEAN ❀ ENERGY FUTURE!

○ Contribute generously to the 401(k) pension or equivalent plan to encourage employee participation.

○ Maintain diversity and gender balance at all levels of the workforce. No excuses.

○ Provide stock options or equivalent forms of company ownership to as broad a base of employees as possible. (Note: Patagonia is wholly owned by the Patagonia Purpose Trust and the Holdfast Collective. No individuals own stock. When they owned the company, Yvon and Malinda Chouinard did not offer stock to employees. They were concerned that, with shares more broadly distributed, the company would become overly cautious in undertaking risk in the pursuit of its environmental goals.)

○ Provide generous vacation pay: one week after six months' employment; two weeks after one year; three and four weeks as soon as possible.

○ Provide paid sick leave and personal days, including bereavement leave, and days to care for sick children.

○ Provide paid maternity and paternity leave for at least ninety days.

○ Allow part-time, flextime, and telecommuting opportunities as appropriate.

○ Install showers so employees can exercise at lunch or bike to work.

○ Establish a relationship with a good childcare center close to work. Better, offer on-site childcare.

○ Ensure that facilities meet Americans with Disabilities Act (ADA) standards or the international equivalent.

○ Provide a company café or kitchen or, if that is not practical, a dedicated space to let employees eat and/or rest.

Patagonia chefs cook up lunch in the café at the
Patagonia Brooks campus, Ventura, California.
TIM DAVIS

○ Subsidize employee travel to work by public transportation or by walking/ biking to minimize the carbon impact of commuting.

○ Provide paid week- to month-long internship opportunities for individual employees to offer their skills to non-profit organizations in alignment with the company's mission.

○ Provide paid sabbatical leave for long-term managerial and creative staff to help prevent burnout.

○ Pay severance to nonexecutive employees who depart in good standing after two years, and specify the amount as a percentage of salary in the employee handbook.

○ Get rid of dehumanizing cubicles; let there be natural light.

○ Publish an employee handbook that details the company's mission as well as its benefits and expectations. It should include a code of ethics, anti-discrimination/harassment policies, and a policy that enables employees to register grievances without fear of reprisal.

○ On an annual basis, conduct a job-satisfaction survey of all employees; quantify and share the results.

○ In a manufacturing or warehouse facility, track all injuries and time lost to injuries.

○ Institute shift-based rather than on-call hiring so families can establish continuity for childcare and sleep routines.

**Element #3:**
**Responsibility to Your Customers**

○ Make long-lasting products whose parts can be repaired.

○ Make useful things that have an identifiable benefit to the user.

○ Make things that benefit the commons.

○ Make things that benefit health or healthy activities (e.g., organic food, mountain bikes, etc.).

○ Make things that benefit artistic or scientific activity (e.g., pianos or astrolabes).

○ Make things that are multifunctional.

○ Vigilantly avoid unnecessary product proliferation (including excessive options, whether of colors or accessories, for popular products).

○ Make environmentally preferable substitutes for environmentally harmful products.

○ Have production or manufacturing processes screened by a third party (e.g., Forest Stewardship Council, Bluesign System Partners, or Leadership in Energy and Environmental Design [LEED]) to reduce environmental harm.

○ Be progressively transparent about the social and environmental impact of what you make. Is anyone in your industry working on a manufacturer- or brand-facing index? Participate in that endeavor.

○ Guarantee your product unconditionally.

○ Serve the underserved; donate what you no longer need to those who do need it. Your company may even get a tax break.

Soon to come tumbling down, whenever the money is found. Matilija Dam, Ojai, California. BEN KNIGHT

**Element #4:**
**Responsibility to the Community**

○ Bank locally where possible—where they know you and you know them.

○ Make opportunities available for lower-income people and people of color in your community.

○ Where possible, provide work for those with physical or learning disabilities.

○ Establish a community service policy. Benchmark and measure performance.

○ Encourage employees to organize group volunteer activities.

○ Create partnerships with local organizations that benefit the environment and the commons.

○ Make your facilities available for use by local organizations outside your working hours.

○ If possible, create a charitable foundation; if your company is too small to do that, give in ways that will make a difference to the communities or causes your company cares about most.

○ Have your charitable giving certified by 1% for the Planet or another branded organization that promotes and vets charitable giving.

○ Identify the major suppliers that represent 80 percent of your purchases. Meet with them annually to mutually review the quality and success of the relationship.

○ Create and maintain an ethics policy for transacting with suppliers.

○ Communicate to your suppliers your company's mission, including your social and environmental standards.

○ Write a code of conduct that identifies your social and environmental standards; insist that your suppliers post your code of conduct where people do significant work on your company's behalf.

○ Set social and environmental standards for your major suppliers.

○ Have third-party services verify whether and how those standards are met. If the standards are not being met, but your supplier is operating in good faith, set goals for continuous improvement in social, environmental, and quality performance; the goals should reflect mutual effort. Benchmark and evaluate performance.

○ Share with other companies what you learn when improving your social and environmental performance so that your industry can follow your lead in establishing best practices.

○ Encourage major suppliers to use renewable energy and to target and track usage.

○ Encourage major suppliers to reduce and monitor greenhouse gas emissions.

○ Encourage major suppliers to reduce waste and divert it from landfill and incinerators and to benchmark and track their progress.

○ Encourage major suppliers to benchmark and reduce water use (and to recirculate or recover water).

○ Mandate the use of wastewater recovery systems by major suppliers.

○ Work with appropriate trade associations to set standards for your industry that reduce social and environmental harm, and to educate consumers on the impacts of the products they buy.

**Element #5:**
**Responsibility to Nature**

○ Conduct independent (if possible) audits of energy and water use, and waste generation. Local utility companies might be helpful with this task.

○ Inventory carbon use. For energy, water, and carbon use, and waste generation, target and measure reductions.

○ Share both targets and results with your board of directors, employees, and other businesses engaged in related activities. Get the word out in staff meetings, company newsletters, suggestion and reward programs, employee manuals, and new-hire orientations.

○ Work with your major suppliers, business partners, and customers to reduce the environmental impact of any activity done in your name. (You can use as a departure point a life-cycle analysis of the 20 percent of your products that generate 80 percent of your sales.)

○ Dedicate a small staff to serve as an environmental resource for business and operational units. Do not create an environmental bureaucracy. Do not subordinate the environmental department to the public-relations or marketing arm of the company.

○ Incorporate environmental goals into job descriptions and performance appraisals, as appropriate.

○ As soon as possible, perform a life-cycle assessment (LCA) of the products that constitute 80 percent of your business.

○ Conduct an independent audit of the toxicity of the major materials used in your products and manufacturing processes—or hire an independent organization like Bluesign that can work directly with your suppliers.

○ Benchmark and target increased use of recycled and biodegradable materials; measure performance.

○ Benchmark and target reductions in packaging.

○ Conduct an independent audit of transportation for all inbound freight. Decrease your use of air and truck shipping; use rail and ocean freight more often. Increase your efficiency; reduce energy use and pollution.

○ Work with your industry trade associations to establish tools that can be integrated into your IT software to measure environmental impact and help improve performance.

○ Take back worn-out products for recycling or repurposing or work with a partner to do so.

○ Design products to be of high quality and lasting value—and with repairable components. The greenest product is often the one the customer doesn't have to replace.

○ Design products to serve as many uses as possible (think cast-iron pan vs. electric can opener).

○ Design products to include as much recycled material as possible.

○ Design products that wear out evenly and whose components can easily be replaced, so that the whole product does not need to be thrown away when a single part fails.

○ Design products that can be recycled and, when possible, made into products of equal value. (It is better that synthetic underwear becomes new underwear, not carpet backing.)

○ Design products with minimal packaging.

○ Monitor energy bills for spikes in use that may indicate the need for maintenance.

○ Buy renewable energy credits.

○ Purchase renewable energy from your utility company.

○ Reduce corporate travel. First- and business-class travel sky-rocket the passenger-per-mile environmental cost.

○ Convert your fleet to electric or hybrid vehicles.

○ Create a vanpool program, if possible.

○ Encourage employees to take the bus or train, carpool, or bicycle or walk to work. Subsidize these alternative transportation methods, if possible.

○ Post to your intranet carpool ride sign-up sheets, bicycle-route maps, and mass-transit schedules/maps.

○ Offer telecommuting opportunities and flexible schedules.

○ Offer lockers and showers for staff who bicycle to work.

○ Provide secure bicycle storage for staff and customers.

○ Provide loaner bikes so employees can do chores or go to doctor appointments without bringing their cars to work.

○ Offer electric-vehicle recharge ports for visitors and staff.

○ Use ceiling fans rather than central air-conditioning units: The fans use 98 percent less energy.

○ Install renewable energy sources, such as solar panels or wind generators.

○ Use a 365-day programmable thermostat to control heating and air conditioning.

○ Convert to heat pump technology.

○ Supplement air-conditioning systems with evaporative coolers on condensers.

○ Set the thermostat to 78°F for cooling, 68°F for heating, and use the thermostat's night setback. If you don't control the temperature, talk to whoever pays the bill. Circulate a letter to everyone sharing the system to suggest how much money could be saved.

○ Seal off unused areas. Block and insulate unneeded windows and other openings.

○ Use small fans or a space heater during off-hours instead of cooling or heating the entire office.

The climbing wall at the Brooks campus of Patagonia gets regular use, Ventura, California. HECTOR VARGAS

○ Use instantaneous water heaters at point of use.

○ Use a solar water heater or preheater.

○ When repainting the building exterior and roof, choose light colors to reflect more sunlight.

○ Build a roof garden.

○ Install and maintain lighting with automatic sleep modes and timers.

○ Use task lighting instead of lighting the entire area.

○ Work with your water company to develop a site-specific "water budget."

○ Monitor water bills for spikes in use. Maintenance may be required.

○ Reduce water pressure to no higher than 50 psi by installing pressure-reducing valves.

○ Replace water-cooled equipment, such as air-conditioning units, with air-cooled equipment or a geothermal heat pump.

○ Irrigate with low-volume, recoverable systems.

○ Harvest rainwater.

○ Irrigate with gray water (from domestic activities such as laundry and bathing) that contains no animal or human waste.

○ Install a self-adjusting, weather-based irrigation controller that automatically tailors watering schedules to match local weather, plant types, and other site-specific conditions.

○ Install matched precipitation-rate sprinkler heads for even distribution of water over a surface area. Avoid runoff onto pavement.

○ Modify your existing irrigation system to include drip irrigation.

○ Install water-flow meters on all large irrigation systems.

○ When repaving parking lots, install permeable concrete or create berms to drain or direct water into plantings.

○ Target zero waste to the landfill or incinerator.

○ Centralize purchasing to eliminate waste and ensure that environmental guidelines are followed.

○ Require the use of low-toxicity cleaning and janitorial products.

○ Design berms, secondary containment, or grading to prevent runoff or rainwater from flowing across industrial and hazardous-liquid storage areas where it could become contaminated.

○ Mulch, or use ground cover, in landscaped areas to prevent exposed soil from washing into storm drains.

○ Regularly check and maintain storm-drain openings and basins. Keep litter, debris, and soil away from storm drains.

○ Keep a spill kit handy to catch/collect spills from leaking company or employee vehicles.

○ Do not use products with added antibacterial agents, such as triclosan; this includes products for handwashing, dish washing, and cleaning.

○ Reduce or replace disinfectants used in industrial processes with environmentally preferable products.

○ Eliminate or reduce pesticides by using integrated pest management (IPM), which includes implementing good housekeeping, acting only when needed, making physical changes to keep pests out, and using fewer or nontoxic pesticides.

○ Keep the kitchen, waste storage, and other areas clean to prevent pest problems.

○ When pest control is necessary, use barriers (such as caulking/sealing holes), traps, and, as a last resort, less-toxic pesticides (such as soaps, oils, microbials, and baits). Apply only as needed (rather than on a routine schedule).

○ Do not allow outdoor perimeter spraying.

○ Purchase organically or locally grown foods and beverages for the lunchroom or café.

○ Use low- or no-VOC (volatile organic compound) paint products.

○ Use natural or low-emission building materials, carpets, and furniture.

○ Replace standard fluorescent lights with no-mercury LED lights.

○ Develop a consumer take-back system (e.g., for printer cartridges) to recover spent products.

○ LEED-certify all construction activities for your facilities. Recycle what you can from demolition, including wood, wallboard, and carpeting.

○ Specify recycled content for carpet and backing, lumber/wood, cabinets, fixtures, drywall, partitions, ceramic and ceiling tiles, roofing, and concrete.

○ Rearrange workspaces to take advantage of areas with natural light, and design for increased natural lighting when remodeling.

○ Use power-management software programs to automatically turn off computers and printers.

NEXT SPREAD  Colleagues work together to solve a
problem in the Patagonia Forge, Ventura, California.
TIM DAVIS

THE CHECKLISTS

○ Serve dishes at office events in reusable serving containers.

○ Eliminate the use of single-serving
disposable water bottles.

○ Compost kitchen waste.

○ Do not use leaf blowers: they blow
particulates around, as well as leaves;
gas-powered leaf blowers cause air
and noise pollution.

○ Leave mowed grass on the lawn for
"green cycling." In dry regions, avoid
lawns in favor of xeriscapes.

# Recommended Reading

Bhatnagar, Urvashi and Paul Anastas
*The Sustainability Scorecard: How to Implement and Profit from Unexpected Solutions*
(Oakland: Berrett-Koehler, 2022)

Chouinard, Yvon
*Let My People Go Surfing*
(New York: Penguin Books, 2016)

Fortier, Jean-Martin
*The Market Gardener: A Successful Grower's Handbook for Small-Scale Organic Farming*
(Gabriola Island, B.C.: New Society Publishers, 2014)

Hawken, Paul, ed.
*Drawdown: The Most Comprehensive Plan Ever Proposed to Reverse Global Warming*
(New York: Penguin Books, 2017)

Hiss, Tony
*Rescuing the Planet: Protecting Half the Land to Heal the Earth*
(New York: Vintage Books, 2022)

Honeyman, Ryan and Tiffany Jana
*The B Corp Handbook, Second Edition: How You Can Use Business as a Force for Good*
(Oakland: Berrett-Koehler, 2019)

MacKinnon, J. B.
*The Day the World Stops Shopping: How Ending Consumerism Saves the Environment and Ourselves*
(New York: Ecco, 2021)

Marquis, Christopher
*Better Business: How the B Corp Movement Is Remaking Capitalism*
(New Haven: Yale University Press, 2020)

McLean, Robert and Charles Conn
*The Imperfectionists: Strategic Mindsets for Uncertain Times*
(Hoboken: John Wiley & Sons, 2023)

Polman, Paul and Andrew Winston
*Net Positive: How Courageous Companies Thrive by Giving More Than They Take*
(Boston: Harvard Business Review Press, 2021)

Ohlson, Kristin
*The Soil Will Save Us: How Scientists, Farmers, and Foodies Are Healing the Soil to Save the Planet*
(Emmaus: Rodale Books, 2014)

Orr, David W.
*Dangerous Years: Climate Change, the Long Emergency, and the Way Forward*
(New Haven: Yale University Press, 2016)

Perlin, John
*A Forest Journey: The Role of Trees in the Fate of Civilization*
(Ventura: Patagonia, 2023)

Raworth, Kate
*Doughnut Economics: Seven Ways to Think Like a 21st-Century Economist*
(White River Junction: Chelsea Green Publishing, 2017)

Samuelson, Judy
*The Six New Rules of Business: Creating Real Value in a Changing World*
(Oakland: Berrett-Koehler, 2021)

Sætre, Simen and Kjetil Østli
*The New Fish: The Truth about Farmed Salmon and the Consequences We Can No Longer Ignore*
(Ventura: Patagonia, 2023)

Smith, Bren
*Eat Like a Fish: My Adventures Farming the Ocean to Fight Climate Change*
(New York: Alfred A. Knopf, 2019)

Arsema Thomas creates a poster ("What's the Debate?") in the Patagonia San Francisco, store for that city's 2018 Rise for Climate March, California. MICHAEL ESTRADA

# Acknowledgments

First thanks go to Susan Bell, an extraordinarily dedicated, thoughtful, thorough editor who helped shape the first edition of *The Responsible Company* and kindly agreed to lend her astute eye and ear to a second go. Susan is an author's guardian angel—and the reader's best friend.

It was a joy to work with two esteemed colleagues from the past: the gifted designer Christina Speed and pioneering outdoor photo editor Jane Sievert. Thank you for all you've contributed to this book, and to so many Patagonia books.

Thanks to the lead team at Patagonia Books, Karla Olson and John Dutton, for their care and shepherding of this project. Thanks as well to Sonia Moore, who keeps everything moving.

Thanks to foreign-rights agent Szilvia Molnar at Sterling Lord Literistic for her work over the past decade to get this book in the hands of non-English speakers.

Thanks to publicist Stephanie Ridge at Wild Ridge Public Relations and Joy Lewis, head of Patagonia Retail, for helping to get the word out.

Thanks to fact-checker Marianne Ratcliff, copy editor Robin Witkin, proofreaders Laurie Gibson, Jocelyn Howell, and Kate Wheeling, and indexer Ken DellaPenta.

Thanks to Vincent's working friends John Fullerton of Capital Institute, builder (in all ways) Jonathan Rose, and Stuart DeCew, Executive Director of the Yale Center for Business and the Environment. Thanks also to great teachers: Brad Gentry, Teresa Chahine, Todd Cort, Blair Miller, and Tony Sheldon.

Special thanks to Ryan Gellert, Patagonia's CEO, and Corley Kenna, Head of Communications and Policy, for their ongoing support—and what they bring to the table.

As a decade ago, last to be named, first always: Nora Gallagher and Malinda Chouinard, our respective mates in love, life, and work. Thanks every day for every day.

# About the Authors

Vincent Stanley was with Patagonia at its beginning, and for many years held key roles as head of sales or marketing. More informally, he was the company's long-time chief storyteller. He serves as Patagonia's director of philosophy and is a resident fellow at the Yale Center for Business and Environment.

Yvon Chouinard is the founder of Patagonia and Patagonia Provisions. He learned early in his life as an alpinist, surfer, and fly fisherman the seriousness of the environmental crisis—and then made this the focus of his companies. In 2022, Chouinard and his family transferred their ownership to a nonprofit dedicated to saving the home planet.

### Online Resources

For the endnotes, a teacher's guide, and reader's guide to this book scan the QR code.

ABOVE LEFT  The coauthors in 1974.  GARY REGESTER

ABOVE RIGHT  In 2023.  TIM DAVIS

# Index

**A**

accounting, 101

Action Works, 115

activism, 43, 76–77, 80–81, 84, 86

Adidas, 149

advertising, 109, 111

agriculture

    industrial, 53, 55

    regenerative organic, 53, 83, 84, 145–46

    small-scale, 55, 146

AI (artificial intelligence), 96, 103

air pollution, 92

algae blooms, 17, 33

Amazon, 138

Amos, Gerald, 1, 115

Anderson, Ray, 72

Androscoggin River, 59

antiracism, 84, 86

apparel industry. *See* textile and apparel industries

Arctic National Wildlife Refuge, 115

Arvind, 133–34

autoimmune disorders, 17

**B**

Baggs, Belinda, 113

Barnacle Foods, 141

Bates Manufacturing Company, 60

B Corp certification, 74–76, 101, 111–12, 123, 148

Bears Ears National Monument, 77, 80

Bell & Howell, 91

Ben & Jerry's, 72

benefit corporations, 75–76

Beretta, 71

Bezos, Jeff, 96

Biden, Joe, 77, 80

B Impact Assessment (BIA), 74, 75, 101, 123, 124

biodiversity, 18, 151

B Lab, 74–75, 111, 135

Blue Coal, 47

Blue Ribbon Flies, 43

Bluesign Technologies, 64–65, 75, 135

The Body Shop, 72

Brooks Range, 115

Bt *(Bacillus thuringiensis)*, 50

Burger King, 149

business responsibility. *See also* checklists

    changing nature of, 91–93

    to the community, 112, 114–15, 181–83

    to customers, 109, 111–12, 179

    to nature, 118–21, 183–86, 188–91

    to owners/shareholders, 97–101, 103, 172

    to society, 121

    to workers, 90–91, 103–8, 173, 176, 178

Bustos, Antonio, 85

**C**

Caldor Fire, 15

cancer, 17, 49

Capelli, Mark, 37, 41

capitalism

    effects of, 114

    regenerative, 150

carbon dioxide, 17, 96, 143, 162

Carl Zeiss Foundation, 165

Carter, Dean, 108

Cash, Johnny, 97

Castro, Hector, 38, 102

C40 Climate Leadership Group, 152–53

change

    experimenting with, 125–26

motivations for, 90

in nature, 18

transparency and, 128, 138

checklists

Element #1: Responsibility to Owners/Shareholders, 172

Element #2: Responsibility to Your Workers, 173, 176, 178

Element #3: Responsibility to Your Customers, 179

Element #4: Responsibility to the Community, 181–83

Element #5: Responsibility to Nature, 183–86, 188–91

Chertow, Marian, 149

child care, 38, 41

child labor, 61

chocks, 35–36

Chouinard, Claire, 168

Chouinard, Fletcher, 38, 168

Chouinard, Malinda, 28, 38, 39, 75, 168, 176

Chouinard Equipment for Alpinists, 7, 25, 26, 27, 30, 32, 33, 36, 38, 44, 58, 105, 166

cigarettes, 121

climate change, 17, 22–23, 93, 96, 118, 142–43, 151

climbing, clean, 33, 35–36

Clinton, Bill, 61, 135

coal, 47, 49, 145

collaborations, 72–76

Colorado River, 20, 21

Common Threads Initiative, 66, 69

communities

components of, 112, 114

responsibility to, 112, 114–15, 181–83

competitors, 134–35

construction, LEED standards for, 46

consumers, spending by, 95

COPD (chronic obstructive pulmonary disease), 17

coral reefs, loss of, 18, 21

corporate social responsibility (CSR) reporting, 57

corporations

benefit, 75–76

limited liability for, 91

Cortez, Sea of, 18

Costco, 138

cotton

Bt, 50

environmental impact of, 50, 65

long-staple, 49

organic, 51, 53, 55, 65, 135, 166

price supports for, 120

recycled, 66, 70–71

COVID pandemic, 23, 29, 80, 86, 106–7, 153, 168

Cummins Engine, 91

customers

demands of, 89

educating, 44

gaining and keeping, 109, 111

responsibility to, 109, 111–12, 179

transparency and, 138

types of, 138

Cuyahoga River, 93

D

Dalhousie University, 159–60

dams, 37

Danone North America, 76, 111

deforestation, 36

De Kuyper, 71

desertification, 21, 93

design, environmental impact of, 87

DHL, 46

Dickens, Charles, 59

diseases, environmental source of, 16–17

Dr. Bronner's, 76, 83

Doughnut Economics, 152–53

Dowding, Charles, 146

*Drawdown* (Hawken), 143

Drucker, Peter, 133

Dunbar, Robin, 104

**E**

Earth Conservancy, 47

*The Ecology of Commerce* (Hawken), 72

economy

    circular, 120, 149

    dependence of, on consumer spending, 95

    electrification of, 143, 145

    growth of, 93

education campaigns, environmental, 44

80/20 rule, 123, 125

Eisenhower, Dwight, 81

El Capitan, 35

Eldorado National Forest, 15

electrification, 143, 145

Elkington, John, 100–101

Ellen MacArthur Foundation, 149

Emerson, Ralph Waldo, 15

employees

    child care for, 38, 41

    layoffs of, 105–6

    meaningful work for, 25

    paying, 86, 107–8

    relationship between employer and, 108

    responsibility to, 90–91, 103–8, 173, 176, 178

    standard of living of, 93

    working group size for, 104

    workweek length and, 108

Endangered Species Act, 15

Endo, Cheryl, 168

environmental harm, reducing, 123–31

environmental justice, 84

Environmental Performance Index (EPI), 22

Environmental Protection Agency (EPA), 16, 49, 149

Erewhon, 72

externalities, 99

extinction, 18, 33

**F**

Faber, Emmanuel, 111–12, 115

Fair Labor Association (FLA), 61, 64–65, 75, 135

Fair Trade Certified, 64, 128, 133

Fair Trade USA, 64–65

fish

    forage, 153, 156–57

    land-based farming, 158–60, 161

    open-net-pen farming, 157–58

fishing nets, recycling, 70

Fitz Roy, 4

Fleming, John, 73

flextime, 38, 41

Floyd, George, 86

Footprint Chronicles, 55, 75. *See also* Our Footprint

Ford, Henry, 92

formaldehyde, 49

Fortier, Jean-Martin, 146

foundation-owned businesses, 165

Francis, Pope, 22, 77

Friedman, Milton, 8, 108

Friends of the Ventura River, 37

Frost, Dorene, 38

Frost, Tom, 35

Fullerton, John, 150

Fundy, Bay of, 158

**G**

GDP (gross domestic product), expanding concept of, 100

Gellert, Ryan, 168

Gifford, Kathie Lee, 61

GIOTEX Sustainable Textiles, 123

globalization, effects of, 21

Goleman, Daniel, 123, 130

Gore, W. L., 104

Great Australian Bight, 113

Groupe Danone, 111

growth, 71–72

**H**

Halifax model, 157–60, 162–63

Havercroft, Kirk, 159

Hawken, Paul, 72, 109, 143

Hayek, Friedrich, 108

Heineken, 165

hemp, 53, 55, 166

Henderson, Hazel, 100

Henokiens, 71

Higg Index, 73–75, 124–25

Hill, Julia Butterfly, 44

Holdfast Collective, 11, 165

Hoshi, 71

Hubbard, Hub, 89

Hudson River, 93

Hugo & Hoby, 148–49

Hulahula River, 115

Hutterites, 104

**I**

IBM, 91

Ikea, 149, 165

industrial ecology, 149

Intel, 104

**J**

Jackson, Wes, 81, 83

Johnson, Huey, 153, 156, 163

Johnson & Johnson, 91–92

**K**

Kanawha River, 167

Kant, Immanuel, 150

Katrina, Hurricane, 49

Kennebec River, 93

Kennedy, Gary, 27

Kernza, 10, 81–84, 144

Knox Coal Company, 47

Koe, Rick, 90, 157, 163

Kukelhaus, Fred, 148

**L**

The Land Institute, 144

layoffs, 105–6

Lee, Jeremy, 159

LEED (Leadership in Energy and Environmental Design) standards, 46

Leonard, Annie, 66

Leonardo da Vinci, 99

Levi Strauss, 71, 72

life-cycle analysis, 120

living systems, 150–51

living wage, 86, 107–8

Long Root Ale, 10, 83

**M**

machines, impact of, 91

Maker's Mark, 76

manufacturing

    lost jobs in, 93

    productivity and, 93

    true cost of, 95–97

Mapuche, 44

Marcario, Rose, 83

Market Gardener Institute, 146

marketing, 109, 111

Mars, proposed colonization of, 18, 96

Maslow, Abraham, 60

maternal leave, 38

Mathews, Craig, 43

Matilija Dam, 180

McDivitt, Roger, 31

McDonough, William, 65

McGovern, George, 108

McKibben, Bill, 53

meaningful work, concept of, 25, 87

mercury, 17

metaverse, 96

methane, 156, 162

Mexico, Gulf of, 17

Microsoft, 104

Monsanto/Bayer, 51

Montpetit, Suleyka, 146

Murie, Margaret, 15

Musk, Elon, 96

Myrt's Cottage Café, 46, 97–98

**N**

NAFTA, 59

Natura, 76

nature

    change in, 18

    language and, 118

    responsibility to, 183–86, 188–91

    rights of, 118

needs, hierarchy of, 60

negative income tax (NIT), 108

Nespresso, 76

NetPlus, 70

New Deal, 92

Nichols, Cindy, 31

Nike, 72

Nissan, 130

Nixon, Richard, 15–16, 108

nylon, 50, 66, 70, 166

**O**

Obama, Barack, 77

Oberland Agriscience, 157, 160, 162

Ocean Wise Plastic Labs, 52, 53

O'Driscoll, Sean Villanueva, 34

Ojai Raptor Center, 28

1% for the Planet, 43, 148

Our Footprint, 55–58, 133

Outdoor Industry Association, 135

owners, responsibility to, 97–101, 103, 172

OxyContin, 121

**P**

Pacific Flyway, 156

Pacioli, Luca, 99

pacu, 157

Paris Accords, 22, 77, 142

Patagonia

    activism and, 43, 76–77, 80–81, 84, 86

    as benefit corporation, 8

Boston store, 48, 49

Brooks campus, 168–69, 177, 187

catalogs of, 44

collaborations and, 72–76

cultural change at, 128–29

employees of, 26, 29, 38, 41, 84, 86, 104–7

environmental giving by, 41, 43, 115

Forge, 8, 191

future of, 165–68

Grants Council, 43, 165

growth and, 71–72

New York City stores, 94

original intention for, 30, 32

Our Footprint, 55–58, 133

Provisions, 10, 83, 84, 157, 166

purpose statement of, 8, 10, 75, 81, 142

Purpose Trust, 11, 165

Reno distribution center, 41, 46, 63

San Francisco store, 195

Santa Monica store, 133, 173

similarity of, to other businesses, 32

suppliers of, 58–61, 63–65, 124, 133–34

transparency of, 134–35, 138

Ventura site, 7, 46, 107, 173

wetsuit repair facility, 102

paternal leave, 38

PCBs (polychlorinated biphenyls), 17

Pearl River, 52

Peterson, Luke, 82

PFCs (perfluorinated compounds), 16

pitons, environmental hazards of, 35

plastics, recycling, 162

policy work, 141–42

polyester, 46, 50, 51–52, 65, 66, 70, 166

post-consumerist society, transitioning to, 95–96

precautionary principle, 118

Prince, Kevin, 135

productivity, increases in, 93

profits, 98–99

**R**

rainforest, loss of, 21

Raworth, Kate, 152–53

recycling, 66, 69–71

regenerative capitalism, 150

regenerative organic agriculture, 53, 83, 84, 145–46

regenerative vitality, 151

REI, 90

Resource Renewal Institute, 156

Responsibili-Tee shirts, 129

responsibility. *See* business responsibility

Rise for Climate March, 195

rivers, 21, 37, 118. *See also individual rivers*

Robinson, Doug, 35

robots, 103–4

Rockström, Johan, 18

Rodale, 83

Rolex, 165

Roosevelt, Teddy, 15

rural areas, 146, 148–49

Rutherford, Kate, 11

**S**

Sackler family, 121

St-Onge, Marc, 162

salmon, 37, 76, 157–60, 163

Samsung, 53

Science Based Targets initiative (SBTi), 22, 118

shareholders, responsibility to, 97–101, 103, 172

Skankey, Wayne, 28

Smallfood, 157, 162–63

small-scale businesses, 146, 148–49

Smith & Hawken, 72, 109

society, responsibility to, 121

soil

   enriching, 83, 145–46

   loss of top-, 37, 81

solar energy, 143, 173

Soldier flies, 160

Stafford, William, 127

STAND-L.A., 173

Stockholm Resilience Centre, 150–51

Stone, Christopher, 118

Stratton, Hall, 27

Stroud, Kim, 28

suppliers

   labor practices of, 61, 63–65

   social and environmental impact of, 133–34

   transparency and, 134, 138

   understanding, 112

Susquehanna River, 47

sustainability, 97, 100

Sustainable Apparel Coalition, 73, 135, 136

Sustainable Blue, 157, 158–60, 161

Sustainable Development Goals (SDGs), 22, 77, 142

Sustane Chester, 157, 160, 162


**T**

Taylor, Frederick Winslow, 92

Tesla, 130

textile and apparel industries

   changes in, 58–61

   employees of, 58–61, 63–65

   pollution by, 52

Textile Exchange, 135

30×30 Initiative, 23, 142, 157

Thomas Fire, 77

Thoreau, Henry David, 15

3M, 91

Thunberg, Greta, 22

Timberland, 72

Tin Shed Ventures, 84

Tompkins, Doug, 26

Tompkins, Kristine, 26

"Tools for Grassroots Activists" conference, 42, 43, 86

trade associations, 112, 114

transparency

   advantages of, 134

   change and, 128, 138

   competitors and, 134–35

   customers and, 138

   importance of, 134, 139

   suppliers and, 134, 138

treaties, 141–42

triple bottom line (TBL), 100–101

Trump, Donald, 77, 80, 168

Tuttle Creek, 4

Twain, Mark, 111


**U**

Unbroken Ground, 7

Unilever, 127

United Nations

   Sustainable Development Goals (SDGs), 22, 77, 142

   TBL and, 101

universal basic income (UBI), 108


**V**

Valley of the Gods, 77

LAST PAGE  The Ventura River mouth is a place of biological diversity and recreational opportunity, Ventura,
California.  JIM MARTIN

Varela, Julio, 27

Ventura River, 36–37, 207

Vertical Knits, 62, 129

"Vote the Environment" campaign, 76

**W**

Walmart, 61, 72–73, 138

Wanger, Greg, 160

washing machines, 53

water

    aquifers, 33, 65

    pollution, 52, 92

    textile industry's use of, 52

wetlands, loss of, 21

White, Fred, 94

Whitehead, Alfred North, 18

wilderness, definition of, 15

Wilson, E. O., 23

wind energy, 143

wool, 50, 66

workers. *See* employees

World Bank, 52

world population, growth of, 93

Worn Wear Program, 67, 69, 110, 149, 201

**Y**

Yosemite, 11, 15, 35

Young, Ben, 148–49

**Z**

Zawacki, Gabby, 47

Zuckerberg, Mark, 96